5-MINUTE RECRUITING

USING VOICEMAIL TO BUILD YOUR NETWORK
MARKETING BUSINESS

DAVID M WARD

GOLDEN LANTERN BOOKS

CONTENTS

5-MINUTE RECRUITING

Using Voicemail to Build Your Network Marketing Business

FREE RECRUITING TIPS NEWSLETTER

Get more recruiting tips with my **FREE Recruiting Tips Newsletter**. You'll also be notified when I release new books or have a special offer.

To subscribe, go here:

http://recruitandgrowrich.com/newsletter

HOW VOICEMAIL BECAME MY FAVORITE
NETWORK MARKETING TOOL

When I started in network marketing, I bought a bunch of tools—videos, audios, brochures—and mailed them to prospects. When I followed up, I found that most of them hadn't looked at anything.

I asked prospects to dial into our team's live recruiting call. I asked them to watch an online presentation. I invited them to come to the live business overview.

The result? You guessed it. Most *didn't* dial into the calls, watch the presentation, or show up at the events.

Frustrating.

I knew some of them would be interested, maybe even excited as I had been, if they would just look at something. I called again and left messages. Most people didn't call back.

We're taught that this is normal. Some will, some won't, yada yada, just keep smiling and dialing, but I thought there had to be a better way.

I remembered something I had done in a business I owned before I started in network marketing. I'm an attorney and had built a successful law practice. Based on my experiences, I wrote a marketing course for attorneys, teaching them how they could get more clients and increase their income.

To get leads for the course, I recorded a **one-minute voicemail message** offering a free report that showed attorneys how to get more clients. The report also told them about the course I was selling.

I placed some small classified ads in the back of a few legal publications, promoting the report and the voicemail number. Attorneys called the number, heard my message, and left their contact information. I sent them the report and the report sold them my course.

Over the next few years that one-minute message brought in **tens of thousands** of leads and allowed me to build a multi-million dollar publishing business.

Why couldn't I do something like that in my network marketing business?

Setting up a lead capture message is easy. You record a short message telling prospects something about what you offer and then you promote the message. If prospects like what they hear and want more information, they leave their name, phone number, and email. If they aren't interested, they don't.

Which means you **only** follow-up with people who are interested.

How much time would that save you? How many more distributors could you recruit?

As I was thinking about this, my upline gave me the phone number to another type of recorded message, a "Sizzle Call." I dialed up the number and listened to the five-minute message.

The speaker told his story—his background, why he started in the business, and what he had accomplished. He talked about the company, the products, and how distributors make money. He shared some product success stories. He talked about people on the team who were doing well in the business. He told us what to do to get more information.

It was good. *Really* good.

I started using that sizzle call with my prospects. (I'll show you how I did this later). After they heard the message, I asked them if they wanted more information. If they didn't, I thanked them and moved on. If they did want more information, I invited them to see the full presentation, review the website, dial into an upcoming conference call, or come to a business briefing.

And they **did it.** They watched the videos, dialed into the calls, and came to the events.

Not because I asked them to because they **wanted** to. They had heard the sizzle call, they were interested, and they wanted to know more.

I started signing up distributors. Later, I recorded my own sizzle calls and signed up even more. I even signed up prospects **using nothing but my story and a 5-Minute sizzle call.**

Sizzle calls quickly became my primary recruiting tool. They helped me recruit **hundreds** of distributors and become a top recruiter and top money-earner in my company.

In this book, you'll learn how to create and use recorded messages to build your network marketing business. You'll learn how to use them to get more leads and how to recruit those leads quickly and with less effort.

WHY NOT USE THE INTERNET?

Some people say you can do all of this online. You can drive traffic to a landing page or other web page where prospects can opt-in to your email list and get information about what you offer. You can send them the information, follow-up, and recruit them (or sell your products), using nothing but email.

In my experience, it's not that simple.

There's nothing wrong with using the Internet to capture leads, deliver information, and follow-up with prospects. I do that, too. But recorded voicemail messages offer some big advantages.

First, most distributor websites and tools (provided by the company) do a lot of "telling" but very little "selling". They focus on the product and the company, not the prospect and what's in it for them. They provide lots of information but they don't do a good job of persuading prospects to take the next step.

With a recorded voicemail message, **you** control the content. You can tell prospects what you want them to know and leave out everything else.

If your distributor website isn't persuasive, your recorded message can tell them what's in it for them and **pre-sell** them on your business or products.

Most people who visit a website offering a business opportunity are skeptical. They know that many things on the Internet are literally too good to be true. When they visit a website, they are conditioned to look for reasons to say no, to *confirm* what they already believe.

It's called "confirmation bias," which is "the tendency to search for, interpret, favor, and recall information in a way that confirms one's preexisting beliefs or hypotheses".

If someone believes that most business opportunities are scams, for example, when they visit your website, they will look for evidence to confirm what they believe. In other words, they'll look for reasons to say no.

When a prospect listens to your sizzle call first, however, and they like what they hear, when they visit your website they may still be skeptical but instead of looking for reasons to say no, they are more likely to look for reasons to say yes.

The second advantage of using voicemail messages is that they allow you to capture leads and do exposures on the fly.

Not everyone has access to the Internet when you connect with them, or the time to watch a full presentation. But most people have their phone with them, which means that if they have five minutes, you can do a quick exposure.

On the phone, it's just you and your message. On the Internet, prospects have too many other options and distractions.

The phone is also more intimate. Even though they may not actually be speaking to you, they hear your voice, your name, and your story. They know you're a real person. When you follow-up, your name and voice are familiar, making it more likely that they will speak to you.

On top of this, you can record a voicemail message in a few minutes and start using it immediately. You don't need any special knowledge, technology, or training.

And you can set up as many voicemail messages as you want, *free* or at very low cost.

Why use a *recorded* message? Because prospects are **three times more likely** to call a recorded message as a regular phone number because they know they can just listen and not speak to someone trying to sell them something.

BUILDING FASTER

Shortly after I heard my first sizzle call, my upline told me he used that message with a network marketing "heavy hitter" who was looking for a new company. Apparently, Mr. Hitter had never used sizzle calls in his business.

When he heard the sizzle call, my upline said that Mr. Hitter was excited. He said, "If ***all I have to do*** is get people to listen to that message, I'm going to *crush* this business!"

He knew that if he got his contacts to listen to the message and they sign up and show it to *their* prospects, in a single evening his team could sign up *dozens* of distributors, with everyone using the same five-minute message.

Sure, this was a network marketing leader talking to other network marketers he's worked with. Most prospects need to see more information before they'll join your team.

But not everyone. I've signed up more than a few prospects using a 5-minute sizzle call, thus the title of this book. I'll show how in Chapter 7.

RECRUITING PROFESSIONALS

If you've read my other books, you know that I recruit a lot of professionals. Having my own recorded messages makes this much easier.

I recorded messages for attorneys. I recorded messages for real estate brokers. I had an insurance agent on my team record a message for insurance professionals.

You can do that, too.

In fact, you can record messages for any niche market: teachers, retirees, college students, network marketing pros, stay-at-home moms, military, professional athletes, clergy, coaches—or any other niche.

Niche-specific messages work better than generic messages because they are tailored to the issues and hot buttons of the specific niche. You can talk about their problems (and your solutions), use their buzz words, and tell success stories about people who come from the same background.

Want to recruit doctors? Have a physician on your team or in your upline record a sizzle call, speaking to their colleagues about what the business means to them.

SELLING MORE PRODUCTS OR SERVICES

Recorded messages aren't just for recruiting. You can also use them to sell your products or services:

- You can record a lead capture message describing the benefits of your product and offer a free sample. (See Chapter 1 for a sample script.)
- You can record messages about new products or special promotions your company is offering.
- You can record "testimonial" messages, where customers or distributors describe how your products have helped them.
- You can record a message that explains why your product(s) are better than anything else on the market.

You can use recorded messages to get new customers, get existing customers to sign up for auto-ship or try your *other* products, or get old customers to order again.

MORE WAYS TO USE RECORDED MESSAGES

There are many other ways to use recorded messages in your business. You can record:

- Testimonials for the business, with top money-earners telling their stories
- A "Frequently Asked Questions" message, to answer questions and overcome objections
- A "first steps" training message for new distributors; have them listen as soon as they sign up
- Other training messages: understanding the comp plan, how to do an exposure, how to do a three-way call, etc.
- "Team news"—a weekly message to your team telling them about new products, upcoming events, current promotions, recruiting tips, motivational messages, interviews, or anything else
- Replays: record your team calls, training calls, corporate messages, calls promoting upcoming events, etc.

WHY I WROTE THIS BOOK

In my first two network marketing books, I talk about how I use recorded messages to build my business. But many distributors don't have access to high-quality messages and don't know how to create them.

I wrote this book to fill that gap, to show you how to create effective recorded voicemail messages, and how to use them. You'll learn

- How to write scripts that get prospects to say, "I'm interested —tell me more". In this book, you get sample **SCRIPTS**, including actual scripts I've recorded and used in my business.
- How long to make your messages—what's too long? What's too short?
- Where to get a **free voicemail** account for your messages— the service I use and recommend
- The easiest, "low tech" way to record your messages
- How to promote your lead capture message—what I do and recommend (including scripts)
- Tracking your numbers—what's a "good" response, how to make it better
- How to use sizzle calls to find interested prospects quickly— the <u>exact</u> method I use
- How to get your first message set up in **one hour or less**

This book is divided into four parts:

Part 1: Lead Capture Messages: Sample scripts and step-by-step instructions for creating your own messages.

Part 2: Sizzle Calls: More scripts, and a simple way to create the ideal message for your business.

Part 3: Recording and Promoting Your Messages: How to set up your voicemail account, how to record your messages, and how to promote and use those messages.

Part 4: How to leave a Voicemail Message That Gets Prospects to Call You Back: When you should (and shouldn't) leave a message on the prospect's voicemail or answering machine, and what to say if you do.

Part 5: Quick Start Guide A step-by-step checklist of everything you need to get started.

Simply put, this book shows you everything you need to know to create and use recorded messages to get more leads (and better leads), recruit more distributors, and build a successful network marketing business.

PART I

LEAD CAPTURE MESSAGES

Most network marketers buy leads from a list broker or lead company. There's nothing wrong with that but the leads you get are usually also sold to distributors in other network marketing companies. That means you're competing with those distributors to recruit the same prospects.

When you have your own lead capture line, you don't have to show prospects why your company offers a better opportunity.

The leads you create with your lead capture message are also better leads those you buy from a list company because the prospects already know something about you and what you offer. They've heard your name and your voice and they know you will be contacting them.

Unlike purchased leads, you won't hear, "Where did you get my name and number!" or "Take me off your list!"

Getting leads with your own lead capture message is a simple three-step process:

Step 1: Set up a voicemail account. In Chapter 5, you'll learn about the free service I recommend.

Step 2: Record a short message. Offer information, a product sample, or something else prospects are likely to want. At the end of the message, tell callers what to do to get (leave their name, phone number, etc.)

You'll learn what to say and what to offer in Chapters 1 and 2.

Step 3: Promote your voicemail phone number. You'll learn the best ways to do that in Chapter 6.

Collect your leads, send them the information you promised, and recruit them.

CHAPTER 1: SAMPLE LEAD CAPTURE MESSAGE SCRIPTS

I n this chapter, you'll see examples of seven different lead capture message scripts, along with comments about when and how you might use them.

The first script is about as simple as it gets. Depending on how you promote your message line, it may be all you need.

The second script (offering a free report) is probably the one you'll use most often.

Note that none of these scripts mention the name of the company or any products or services. That's because if you give this information to prospects on a lead capture message, many prospects won't leave you a message. They'll hang up and research you online. They might find negative information about your company but you won't be available to explain it. Or they might find another distributor's website and sign up with them.

Never mention the name of your company or your products on your lead capture message.

You want to make people curious so they'll leave their contact information, not satisfy their curiosity before you have a chance to talk to them.

Read through these scripts, get some ideas, and in the next chapter, you'll learn how to create a script for your business.

SCRIPT: THE "THANKS FOR CALLING" MESSAGE

Most lead capture messages are brief—one to two minutes in length. Sometimes, even less. That's because the purpose of these messages isn't to persuade prospects to buy anything or sign up for anything, it is simply to get them to leave their contact information.

The simplest type of lead capture message doesn't provide any information about what you do or what you offer. It simply prompts the caller to leave their contact information in order to receive information or something else offered elsewhere—in an ad, article, post, presentation, handout, etc.

Your ad or handout tells the prospect what you have for them—a method for making money on the Internet, a simple way to earn money from home, information about your amazing product, a way to stop a painful or expensive problem, or anything else you offer. Your message thanks them for calling and tells them to leave their contact information.

Nothing else.

The caller is given no other information. They don't know who you are or how to contact you. If they want what is being offered in your ad or article, they have no choice but to leave a message.

Here's the script:

"Hello and thank you for responding to our advertising [marketing] campaign. At the sound of the tone, please leave your name, address, telephone number and email and one of our representatives will contact you as soon as possible."

Does something like this really work? Sure. If the caller wants what you've promised him in your ad or promotional material, she will leave her information.

One network marketing expert who uses this script says that according to his tests, this script works **better than anything else** he has tried. He says he has testimonials from hundreds of distributors who told him that when they switched to this script, their response rate went up dramatically.

A few comments about this script:

- For this to work, your ad or article has to convince the prospect to not only call your message line but to leave their contact information. If it does that, a brief "thanks for calling" type of message may be all you need.
- The effectiveness of this type of message may depend on who you are targeting in your ad or other materials. Some types of prospects, e.g., professionals, business owners, or experienced network marketers, might need to know more about what you're offering before they are willing to leave a message. If that information isn't supplied in your ad or promotional material, this might not be the right type of message for you.
- The message tells them that *a representative will contact them.* This might lower response but it will also mean you won't

waste time calling people who won't answer or return your call. In other words, you may get fewer leads but they will be better leads.

I'll have more to say about this type of message in Chapter 2.

SCRIPT: THE "FREE REPORT" MESSAGE

I mentioned earlier that when I was marketing my course to attorneys, I offered to send prospects a "Free Report" that showed them how they could get more clients. To get the report, the ad told them to dial a toll-free number and listen to a "24-hour Free Recorded Message".

On the message, I introduced myself and briefly told my story. I said that when I started my law practice I had a hard time getting clients and paying my bills. I told them how rough it was my first few years. Then I said that I was finally able to turn things around by learning some marketing skills and I used these to build a successful practice.

I offered to send them a free copy of my report. All they had to do was leave their name, address, and phone number. I also asked them to indicate the type of law they practiced and where they saw my ad.

The message was approximately 75 seconds long.

Attorneys called the voicemail number, listened to my message, and left their contact information. I sent them the report and information about my marketing course and followed up and sold them my marketing course.

The message worked because

- Callers heard my story, in my own voice. I was their colleague, not an actor or salesperson, and I had "been in their shoes," e.g., wanting to bring in more clients but not knowing how to do it.
- I used a toll-free 800 number, which meant they didn't have to pay for the call. This resulted in more calls, but you probably don't need to use a toll-free number today.
- The message was recorded and available 24-hours a day. Prospects could call at any time, night or day, and listen to the message, knowing they didn't have to talk to anyone.
- I offered information about how to get something I knew they wanted.
- I didn't try to sell them anything on the message, or even tell them about the course I was selling. I merely offered to send them my free report, with no cost or obligation.

The call was free, the report was free and promised a valuable benefit. How could they refuse?

It works the same way in a network marketing business.

You record a message telling prospects how you (or someone you know) increased your income or otherwise improved your life, and you offer callers a report (or something similar—see below) so they can learn how to achieve the same benefits.

Here is a sample script offering a free report, based on a message I used in my network marketing business.

SAMPLE SCRIPT: ARE YOU LOOKING FOR A PLAN B?

"Hello and thanks for calling. My name is David Ward and I live in Orange County, California. I don't know where you are in life right now but if you're looking for a way to earn more income or you need a Plan B, I think you're going to like this message.

A lot of people today are thinking about starting a business but they don't do it because they don't have the tens of thousands or hundreds of thousands of dollars it takes to start most businesses. Or, they have the money but they don't have the time.

I know the feeling. It wasn't long ago that I was a very busy and very stressed out attorney. I practiced law for over twenty years and had a great career but I was always working and never had enough time for my family or anything else and I finally realized that if I didn't make some changes in my life, the next twenty years would probably turn out pretty much the same. That's when I began looking for a Plan B.

Because I was so busy, I needed to find something I could do part time but had the potential to provide a full-time income. I looked at a lot of different options but everything I looked at was either too time-consuming, too risky, or just plain silly. I kept looking and eventually found something that made sense and I got started, just a few hours a week.

Within a few months, I was earning thousands of dollars a month in extra income. It wasn't long before I was earning six figures, and I did it working part time, a few hours a week. Today, my Plan B has turned into my Plan A —I no longer practice law but I still earn a healthy six-figure income, only now, I have time to spend with my family, to travel, and do things I didn't have time to do before.

If you'd like to do something fun and challenging and financially rewarding, something that can generate an income of five or ten thousand dollars a month, or even a lot more, I can show you how. You don't need any particular talent or business experience, you don't need a lot of money, and you can get started, like I did, with only a few hours a week.

If that sounds good to you and you'd like to get some information, go ahead and leave your name, telephone number and email at the end of this message. I'll send you a copy of a report entitled, "How to work smarter and retire sooner." The information in this report changed my life and it can do the same for you. Again, leave your name, phone number, and email and I'll get the report out to you as soon as possible. Thanks again for calling."

WHAT IF YOU DON'T HAVE A REPORT?

Your company or upline might have something you can send to prospects:

- Information about how to start a home-based business, earn money from home, or how to choose the right network marketing company
- A guide to [buying supplements, whatever you sell], investing, improving health, weight loss, etc.
- A "planning guide," checklist, ebook, or instructions for accomplishing something important related to your business or products
- Anything else that can help them improve their life related to what you do

If there's nothing available, you can create something yourself without doing any writing. If you market health-related products, for example, you could gather together several articles on health-related topics related to what you do. Find some articles online, put them in a pdf, and highlight anything you want prospects to note.

On the other hand, your "report" can be *anything*—a webinar or online video about your products and business, a replay of a live conference (e.g., your weekly recruiting call), or your website.

Am I saying that you can use the same recruiting tools you already use in your business?

Yes.

As long as your "report" delivers the information you promised — a solution to a problem, a way to earn more income, advice on starting a home-based business — it doesn't matter what form it's in.

SCRIPT: "CONSUMER AWARENESS MESSAGE"

The "consumer awareness" message alerts prospects to a problem or issue they currently have or might develop, e.g., bad health, obesity, debt, overpaying for insurance, identity theft, and so on.

Your message **warns** them about the problem and the risks they face if they ignore it.

If you sell nutritional supplements, for example, your message might warn about the dangers of taking a common type of supplement, or about not taking a supplement they need. You would then offer them additional information about this problem and how to deal with it.

Let's say you sell air filtration systems and you run an ad warning people about the dangers of breathing "indoor" air. You offer to send them a free research report that shows them what they need to know to stay safe and healthy.

AIR FILTRATION CONSUMER AWARENESS MESSAGE

"Hello and thanks for calling. If you're concerned about the quality of the air you breathe and how it affects your health, well, frankly, you should be. Research shows that the air in many US cities contains dozens of pollutants

and is responsible for a dramatic increase in asthma, allergies, and breathing problems in adults and children alike. Even worse, the air inside your home can have as much as 5 times more pollutants than the air outside.

If you'd like to get a free report about this research and learn how an air filtration system can help protect you and your family from these dangers, please leave your name, address, phone number and email at the end of this message. Speak clearly and repeat the information twice. Your free report will be sent to you immediately, along with a special gift. Start recording after the beep. . ."

[Note—I made up the "bad air" information but I wouldn't be surprised to learn that it's not far from the truth. The "special gift" you send could be a discount coupon and/or referral cards they can pass out to friends and get referral fees when someone they refer buys one of your units.]

A consumer awareness message is similar to the "Free Report" message. But while the free report message usually promises an affirmative benefit, e.g., extra income, time freedom, working from home, *a consumer awareness message focuses on alerting the prospect to a problem they know about and want to stop or prevent, or a problem they DON'T know about that poses a danger.*

This type of message can be used when you lead with your product or service, as in the message above, but it can also be used if you lead with your business opportunity.

For example, you might run a consumer awareness message about the dangers of failing to save enough money for retirement. On your message, you might quote articles about how little social security pays, how much it costs to retire, why you can't count on a pension, and so forth. You promise to send callers information about a way you discovered for creating passive income that may eventually allow them to retire, (your business opportunity).

SCRIPT: THE "FREE SAMPLE" MESSAGE

If you offer prospects free samples of your products or a "free trial" of your service, you can feature that offer on a lead capture message.

Your message should reference a problem the caller wants to solve or prevent, describe what your product does, i.e., the benefits customers get when they use or consume it, and offer to send them a free sample, with no obligation to buy anything.

Your message might also tell them how the product works and why it's better than competing products.

You might explain why you are making this offer — "as part of a special promotion," "to celebrate the launch of our new market," or, simply, "to get the word out about this amazing product."

But remember, don't tell them the name of your product or company.

There are two ways you can "position" yourself in this kind of message. The first is to take yourself out of the picture. Don't mention your name, don't say, "I will send you," say, "*we* will send you," and make the message sound like a company is running the promotion.

Callers may trust the message more if they think they're dealing directly with "the company".

The other way to do it is just the opposite. Introduce yourself and (briefly) tell your story. Talk about the problem you or someone you know had, and what the product did for you (them) or what it means to you. [If you sell nutritional products, make sure you follow company guidelines when speaking about "results," "cures," "guarantees," and so on.]

The advantage of putting yourself in the picture is that prospects can see you as a real person and a satisfied customer, not a nameless salesperson or paid actor. You might get a higher percentage of callers to leave their contact information because of this.

In addition, when you contact the prospect, they may feel like they "know" you to some extent because they've heard your name, your voice, and your story. This might make them more likely to take your call, and more likely to buy or join.

Go with the approach that feels right to you, or try it both ways and see which one works best.

Here is an example of a script using the personal approach.

'FREE SAMPLE' SCRIPT FOR NUTRITION PRODUCT

"Hi and thanks for calling. Are you and your family getting all the vitamins and minerals you need? Do you have as much energy today as you did a few years ago? My name is Samantha Stevens and about a year ago I realized that I seemed to be tired all the time. I couldn't get through the day without drinking coffee in the afternoon. Sometimes, I had to take a nap. My doctor told me to take a vitamin supplement, and I did but it didn't seem to help. Then I heard about a new type of supplement that came in liquid form and has all the vitamins, minerals, probiotics, and Omega 3 fish oil missing from most people's diets.

The woman's blend has special herbs to balance hormones; the men's formula is formulated to support a healthy prostate.

I started taking the woman's formula a few months ago. Today, I have a lot of energy and I feel great. I was so excited about what this product has done for me, I signed up as a distributor for the company. I'd like to send you a free 5-day supply of our energy formula to try for yourself. No shipping, no monthly charge, and no credit card is required. Just leave your name, complete mailing address, phone number and email. Speak clearly and repeat the information twice. Oh, and if you know anyone who would like to earn some extra income by helping to share this great product, let me know. I'll send you a nice gift to say "thank you". Thanks again and have a great day. Start recording after the beep. . ."

SCRIPT: THE "FREE DRAWING" MESSAGE

A great way to get prospects to leave their contact information is to offer them a gift or the opportunity to win a prize in return for doing so. You can offer the gift for simply leaving their information when they register for your upcoming webinar, or for attending a live business presentation.

The gift might be a package of your products or free samples plus discount coupons. Contact local hotels, restaurants, spas, and other businesses and see if they are willing to offer a voucher for free or discounted services, as a way to promote their business. You could also do a search for "travel vouchers" or "gift vouchers".

Instead of giving everyone a free gift, you could enter the names of everyone who leaves their information (or comes to your showcase) into a drawing for a prize. This could be a free month's worth of your products or services, for example, or something like an iPad.

Careful, though. Drawings and giveaways must comply with the laws of the states and countries in which you are promoting them, and there are strict penalties for violating those laws. Check with your company (or an attorney), to find out the laws in your jurisdiction.

Here's a sample script that offers callers a "free gift" for attending your 'open house':

SAMPLE SCRIPT

Hi and thanks for calling. Are you concerned about [problem or issue your products or services address]? It's a big problem today. Unfortunately, many people don't know what to do/how to prevent it/how to protect themselves from . . .

If you would like to [general benefit, e.g., improve your overall health/protect yourself and your family/etc.] we can help.

We'd love to send you two tickets to our upcoming [WORKSHOP/PRESENTATION/OPEN HOUSE] to learn more. You'll also receive a special gift for attending — a voucher for a free appetizer and drinks for two at Martin's Steak House. There's nothing to purchase—this is our gift to you for attending our workshop. Leave your name, address, phone number and email address at the end of this message and we'll send you details about the next workshop, and your appetizer and drink vouchers for you and a guest. . .

If you're offering a drawing, use this version:

We'd love to send you two tickets to our [WORKSHOP/PRESENTATION/OPEN HOUSE] and enter your name in our monthly drawing for [prize].

Please leave your name, complete mailing address, phone number and email. Speak clearly and repeat the information twice. Thank you.

Optional: *If you know anyone who would like to earn extra income by helping us share this information, please refer them to this message. Make sure they mention your name and we'll have a nice gift for you. And YES— you can refer yourself! Thanks again—start recording after the beep.*

SCRIPT: "ARE YOU THE ONE WE'RE LOOKING FOR?"

Here's a sample script for a business opportunity lead capture message, designed to appeal to the caller's ego.

SAMPLE SCRIPT—ARE YOU THE ONE WE'RE LOOKING FOR?

"Hello and thanks for calling. My name is John Martin and for the last several years my team and I have been helping people just like you earn more income in their own home-based business. Thousands of people credit their success to the wealth-building systems my partners and I have put together.

Now, it's your turn.

I'd like to send you some information about our company and our wealth-building program. There is no cost or obligation. Look at the information, see what we do, see how much you can earn and decide if this is for you.

Our program is simple, it's powerful, and most important, it really works. You can do this part time or full time. You don't need any prior business experience and you won't be asked to invest a lot of money. We don't need your money, we need your sincere desire to make a change in your life and the willingness to put in some time and effort. We'll teach you everything you need to know and we'll help you every step of the way.

But, our program isn't for everyone. It may not be for you. Only you can decide that, after you look at the information.

Now, I know what you're thinking. You're thinking this is a scam or a crazy get rich quick scheme. I assure you it is not. Our company has been in business for more than a decade. We market high-quality products and services and have a triple-A rating with the Better Business Bureau. I'll show you proof of all that, and more, with the information I send.

Why are we offering this program? Because our company is growing quickly and we need help. If you like what you see, we'd like to talk to you about working with us. And again, there is no cost or obligation to look at the information.

If that sounds fair, at the sound of the tone, leave your name, address, telephone AND email address and I'll rush you a complete package. Again, leave your name, address, telephone, and email. Speak slowly and spell your name and email. Thanks again for calling. I look forward to speaking with you."

SCRIPT: "I SWORE I'D NEVER DO NETWORK MARKETING AGAIN"

Unlike many messages, this one doesn't try to hide the fact that you are offering a network marketing opportunity. It is mentioned prominently, to weed out prospects who don't like network marketing and appeal to people who do. Where this type of message really shines, however, is in appealing to people who like network marketing but don't think they can be successful at it.

That was me. I was convinced that I didn't have the temperament for network marketing and after several failed attempts, literally said to myself, "never again". I later learned that many people who have given up on network marketing are actually open to trying again if the right opportunity comes along. Sure enough, when I found the right opportunity, I signed up and built a successful business.

The script for this type of message is essentially a testimonial for your opportunity. Basically, you tell your story.

If this is your first network marketing business, describe what your life was like before and why you wanted to start a business. Tell them some bad things you'd heard about network marketing or the bad experiences some of your friends have had. Then tell them why you finally decided to give it a try and how you're doing in the business.

If you've been with other companies before, tell them why things didn't work out and what's different now. For example, you might say that you weren't successful before because you didn't take the business seriously, you didn't follow the system you were taught, or you didn't give it enough time. Many prospects who have struggled in network marketing will relate to your story.

If you "swore off" network marketing because of one or more bad experiences, say that, followed by what prompted you to change your mind.

Did you meet someone (your current sponsor or upline) who was willing to help you in ways your previous upline wasn't?

Did you fall in love with the products offered by your current company, start telling friends about the products, and realize you might as well get paid for doing that?

Did you watch a friend become successful in your company and convince yourself you should take a look?

Or were you so frustrated with your job, or being out of work, that you were willing to give network marketing another go?

Don't beat up your prior company even if they had some serious issues. Just tell prospects why your current company was a better fit for you. Describe how you're doing now and state that you're glad you didn't let your prior experience stop you from trying again.

SAMPLE SCRIPT FOR NETWORK MARKETING

"Hi and thanks for calling. If you're looking for a new network marketing opportunity, I think you're going to like this message.

My name is Tom Tuttle. A few years ago I started a network marketing business because I wanted to earn more income and be my own boss. Okay, the truth is I wanted to get rich and I thought network marketing was a good way to do it. Unfortunately, I made some bad decisions and failed miserably. Never made more than a few hundred dollars in a month. It was so bad, I gave up. I told myself network marketing wasn't for me and I'd have to find something else.

One day a friend of mine told about a new company he just signed up with. He wanted me to take a look. I was expecting to see the same thing every other company offers and tell him, "It's not for me," but I had to admit, I was impressed. They really seem to know what they're doing.

My friend introduced me to his upline, and he told me about the training and support their team offered. I've never seen anything like it. They have an amazing "field training" approach, with the goal of helping every distributor get to a minimum of $1,000 a month within their first 90 days. They also have a great lead program. If a distributor wants to build fast, they've got the leads to help them do it.

Anyway, I got excited and signed up. And today. . . [results].

I'm sure glad I was willing to look at this business. If you'd like to get some information. . . "

CHAPTER 2: HOW TO CREATE AN EFFECTIVE LEAD CAPTURE MESSAGE

I n the first chapter, you saw examples of different lead capture message scripts. Which one should you use?

If this is your first lead capture message, I recommend using a "Free Report" message.

The key to this type of message is to tell prospects how they will be better off by reading your report. How will they benefit from the report? What will they learn?

Will they learn how to earn extra income working from home? Will they learn how to create passive income that can help them retire some day? Will they learn how to start an Internet business and make money working one to two hours a day?

Does your report show them an easy way to lose weight, lower their blood pressure, or increase their energy?

Will they find out how to get better drinking water for four cents per gallon so they can get rid of expensive bottled water? Will they learn how to improve the air quality in their home so they can breathe better and avoid common health problems associated with poor air quality?

Tell them what they will learn or be able to do as a result of reading your report.

Make a BIG promise. You want prospects to get excited about what you have for them and look forward to receiving it.

The title of the report I offered to send prospects for my marketing course for lawyers was, *"How to Get More Clients in a Month Than You Now Get All Year!"* This not only promised something they wanted, it made them curious to find out how something like that was even possible. The only way to find out, of course, was to read the report, and the only way to do that was to leave their information.

As noted earlier, my message didn't say anything about the course I was selling. I told them about the report and what it would help them do. The *report* sold them on my course.

You should do the same. Promote your report, not your business or product. Let the report (video, web page, ebook, webinar, etc.) promote your business or product.

WRITING YOUR MESSAGE SCRIPT

Your lead capture message script should contain the following elements:

- **Welcome.** Introduce yourself and tell your story.
- **State the problem.** What problem(s) is the caller likely to have that your products/business can help them with?
- **Agitate the problem.** How bad could it get? What could happen if they don't do something about it or they wait too long?
- **Present the solution.** Tell them about your report or other offer. Describe the benefits. *Don't mention the name of your company or products.*

- **Call to action.** Tell them what to do to get it.

YOUR STORY

On a lead capture message, you won't have much time to tell your story, but you want to tell callers something about yourself so they can relate to you and trust you enough to leave their contact information.

Give them an abbreviated form of your testimonial:

- **Your name and background.** What you do for a living, or what you did before.
- **Your (previous) problem or situation.** What you wanted and why.
- **Your current situation.** What problem did you solve? What have you accomplished or are you on your way to accomplishing?

No matter what your situation, even if you're just getting started with the products or the business, you can always tell a good story. You started your business for a reason—what was it? Tell callers what motivated you to do something about your problem or situation and they will see themselves in your story.

If you don't yet have any significant results, tell callers that you are "on track to. . . [accomplishing your desired results]. What callers care about is what's possible for them. Telling them what you're working towards is usually enough to show them what's possible for them.

If you want more, talk about someone else in the business who has those results, someone who inspired you to start your business or start using your products. Bring them into your story by saying, "I met someone who. . ." and describe what they told you or what you saw.

Your story, any story, can be told in as little as one or two sentences.

THE CALL TO ACTION

At the end of your message, you will tell callers to leave their name and other information after the "tone" or "beep". This is referred to as the "call to action".

What information do you want them to give you?

At a minimum, you want their name and phone number. If you plan to mail something, you'll need their physical mailing address. But if prospects wish to protect their privacy asking for their address might lower response so don't ask for it unless you really need it.

What about email? You'll need this to send them a download link for your report, links to websites and videos, for follow-ups, and so on, so yes, you need their email.

Some prospects might tell you that the best way to contact them is by email and omit their phone number. Others may give you a bogus phone number. Most people will follow your instructions, however, and provide the information you ask for, including their phone number.

If someone doesn't leave a phone number, or they leave a bogus number, you can send them an email and tell them you have their report (or whatever), but you need to speak with them briefly to verify some information before you send it. In my opinion, you need to talk to prospects, for reasons I explained in *Recruit and Grow Rich*. Tell them to reply with their phone number and the best time to reach them.

If they don't provide a phone number, you have to decide if prospects who won't talk to you are worth your time. Me? I move on. If they don't want to talk to me, I don't want to talk to them. Next.

They may reconsider at some point and call your message line again and leave their number. They may realize they still don't have your report or the free sample or whatever you offered them and still want it, so they call again.

I've had that happen. It's a beautiful thing.

If a high percentage of callers don't leave their phone number or leave a bad number, you should probably re-do your message. Instead of telling them to leave their phone number, say, "Please leave your BEST phone number and the best time to reach you," to make it clear you will be calling. If you're still getting a lot of bad numbers, add something like this:

"No information [sample, etc.] will be provided without a valid phone number".

CALL TO ACTION FOR NETWORK MARKETING SCRIPT

In a script targeting network marketing distributors, you may want to use a more aggressive call to action than the typical, ". . .please leave your name and number. . ."

Here are some options:

- I'll call you: "Leave your name and phone number, I'll give you a quick call, we'll chat for a few minutes and I'll show you what I have to offer. No more than five minutes. If it takes longer than that, it will be your fault, not mine. I'm not going to try to sell you anything or convince you to do anything; I'll simply show what you what I've done and what others have done and see if it sounds like a good fit for you. There's no cost or obligation and I'm not going to spam you or annoy you so leave your name and number and email and the best time to reach you and I'll be in touch. Thanks again and I'll talk to you soon."
- You call me: If you have a great story and great "music," or you are targeting a niche market that will relate to you and your story (e.g., because you have the same background, occupation, or type of business), tell prospects to call YOU if they want to hear what you offer. You give the caller no other option. If they want to learn more, they have to call. You'll get

a lot fewer leads but the ones who call you will no doubt be motivated.

- Heavy hitter: ". . .I am a top executive with our company. For the last four years, our team has helped thousands of people to earn extra income, part-time from home. Hundreds of people have been able to replace the income from their job and go full time with our company. And more than two dozen distributors on our team are earning six-figure incomes; some are earning seven-figures. Many on our team started with no experience in network marketing. They were successful because they were hungry, they were coachable, and they were willing to do the work. How about you? Let me send you some information so you can see what we do and if you like what you see, we'll set up a time to talk."
- We'll work with you: ". . .I get a lot of calls and obviously, I can't work with everyone. If you are accepted into the program, I want you to know we won't just sign you up and abandon you. My team and I will help you get your business started and we'll help you earn as much income as possible as quickly as possible."
- Why you?: ". . .I get a lot of calls and obviously, I can't work with everyone. If you'd like to be considered, tell me why I should work with you." This puts yourself in a position of power and you might be surprised at how people respond.
- Three questions: "If you can answer yes to the following three questions, go ahead and leave your contact information and we'll get an information package out to you.

Question 1: Would you be willing to spend 5 to 10 hours a week working with me and our team and follow our proven 7-step success system, if you knew you could be successful at this?

Question 2: As you know, it can sometimes take thousands of dollars to launch a new business from scratch. However, you can get started with our system for about $100-$300. Is your financial freedom important enough to commit to investing this amount to get started?

Question 3: On a scale of 1 to 10, with 1 being 'I'm just window shopping' and 10 meaning 'I'm extremely motivated,' how would you rate your level of interest at this time?

If your interest is at least a 6, I invite you to leave your name, address, phone number, and email address, and we'll send you a free information package."

OPTION: TELL ME ABOUT YOURSELF

At the end of the message, before the call to action, you might ask the caller to leave additional information about themselves—their experience, their current situation or challenges, their goals, or their preferences.

For example, "To get a free copy of our guide to choosing a home-based business, at the end of this message, please leave your name, telephone number, and email, and tell me a little about your experience with a home-based business, or the type of business you're interested in."

This will give you a place to start when you call: "I see you tried Internet marketing at one point. How did that work out for you?" You can then show them how your business is a better way for them to get what they're looking for.

In addition, when a prospect tells you about their experience or current interest, they often feel connected to you because they've opened up and shared something personal about themselves. Because of this, they may be more likely to take your call, and more likely to keep an open mind about what you show them.

KEEP IT SHORT, KEEP IT SIMPLE

If this is your first attempt at writing a script, your best bet is to re-write one of the sample scripts in the previous chapter. If you have access to a lead capture message used by another distributor, with your company or another network marketing company, rewriting their message is another option.

Keep your message short and simple. Talk about one key benefit, not everything. Make them curious to learn more.

Don't go overboard with the excitement or the promises. People can smell hype a mile away and they won't leave a message.

You should be able to cover everything in one or two minutes. That includes approximately 20 seconds for the instructions—telling them what to do, repeating it, and speaking slowly enough so they can follow you. That doesn't leave a lot of time for everything else.

You can go longer. Some of my scripts do. But be careful. You don't want to promise too much or appear to be trying too hard. You don't want callers to stop and think about what you're saying, you want them to get excited and follow your instructions.

ARE YOU READY?

You now know how to write a short script for a lead capture message. If you're ready to set up your message now, skip ahead to Chapter 5 to learn how to set up a voicemail account and record your message.

Then, turn to Chapter 6 to learn how to promote your lead capture message.

On the other hand, Part 2 (about Sizzle Calls) has additional information about writing an effective script and you may want to read this first.

PART II

SIZZLE CALL MESSAGES

Lead generation messages are brief and lacking in details. Remember, they need to tell prospects only enough to get them to request information about what you offer. Sizzle calls are different. They need to provide enough information to persuade callers to take the next step—to meet with you, come to a live presentation, dial into a conference call, watch your video, etc.

A recruiting sizzle call is basically a condensed version of your full business presentation. The speaker acknowledges the prospect's situation and desire to solve a problem or improve their life. They tell prospects about your products or services, your company, and your business opportunity. They tell them how much they can earn in the business and what they will do to earn it. And they tell prospects to sign up or get more information.

They're called "sizzle calls" or "sizzle messages" because they present the *sizzle*, meaning the highlights or big picture, not the "steak" or the details.

Most sizzle calls are under ten minutes, with the majority probably averaging around five minutes. That's long enough to cover the basic information a prospect needs to know to decide if they want to learn more.

You may have access to sizzle calls already in use by distributors in your company. Listen to these messages as a prospect might and ask yourself if they are effective. Do they get you excited about the business?

Talk to some distributors who know about the calls. Do they use them? Are they signing up distributors?

A sizzle call should focus on telling prospects "what's in it for them". It should tell them the benefits of the business, talk about successful distributors, and tell them why they can also be successful. It should provide a few details, not try to tell them everything.

The purpose of the message isn't to inform prospects it is to *persuade* them.

Many sizzle calls don't do that. Instead of talking to the prospect about how they can increase their income, work from home, build retirement income, and help make the world a better place, they talk about the company and the products. Those are important, of course, but prospects want to know why they should become a distributor.

Again, "what's in it for them?"

Read the sample sizzle call scripts in Chapter 3 to get an idea of what a persuasive sizzle call sounds like. Listen to the sizzle calls that are available to you. If they are good, go ahead and use them. At least for now.

At some point, you may want to record your own (or work with someone in your upline or on your team to do that). When that time comes, Chapter 4 will show you what to do.

CHAPTER 3: SAMPLE SIZZLE CALL SCRIPTS

Network marketing companies (and teams) obviously have different products or services, different compensation, and different philosophies about training and building the business. We also have different notions about what to include and what to emphasize on a sizzle. And yet, our prospects generally all want the same things.

The difference is in the details.

As you read the sample scripts in this chapter, think about how they might work in your business if you add details about your products or services, compensation, and method of doing business.

Many of the sample scripts target professional prospects since that's who I focus on in my business. They can be modified to appeal to other types of prospects by adding different benefits such as, "extra income," "be your own boss," or "work from home".

Read the scripts and get some ideas. In Chapter 4, I'll show you how to write a script for your business.

SCRIPT: A WALK AROUND THE LAKE

I once heard a sizzle call being used by a distributor in another company. I liked the call so much I borrowed some ideas and wrote a version for my business.

In the version below, the facts about the company and products are obviously fictitious. As you read this, note the elements you need to modify to reflect your business:

- Facts about the company, positive press
- What the products do [benefits]
- The need for the products [Why people need them, the size of the market, the future for the company
- How you earn money [commissions, overrides, etc., and what you do to earn it]
- Statistics about successful distributors/incomes [make sure you follow state law and company guidelines]

SCRIPT—A WALK AROUND THE LAKE

Hello, my name is David Ward and I want to thank you for taking the time to listen to this message. In the next few minutes, I'm going to give you some information that will get you thinking about your future. I'm recording this message at 2 o'clock on a Tuesday afternoon. I actually started at 8:30 this morning but I was interrupted when my wife Kathy asked me to join her for a walk around the lake near our home in southern California. I said "let's go", and in a few minutes, we were at the lake, admiring the ducks and the geese on the water and the mountains in the distance, and on the way back home, we stopped for breakfast at a nearby cafe.

Remember this is Tuesday. If you're like most people, you don't get to do this. I don't mean walk around a lake, I mean you don't get to leave your work whenever you want to, to do something really important, like spending time with your family, and until a few years ago, I wasn't able to take off whenever I felt like it either, because I worked long hours as an attorney and for over twenty years I was always at the office or in court or stuck in traffic. My career kept me busy and my other needs just had to wait and if you have a corporate career or a business or a job or you're a professional, you know the trade-off. The question is ,is the trade off really worth it?

No, it's not worth it.

Making big money means nothing unless you have time to enjoy it, but there's a premise in our society that says you can't be successful and have free time to enjoy your family, your friends, your hobbies or the pursuit of happiness and I say this is an obsolete premise.

Whether you're self-employed or you have a job, the reason you don't have financial freedom and the reason you don't have time freedom is because you exchange your time for dollars and no matter how hard you work, there are only so many hours in a day. Working hard is not the answer. Most people work hard all their lives and have very little to show for it, and that's because most people were never taught the mechanics for creating wealth. Leverage is the key to wealth and leverage is the key to time freedom, but of course you need to find a leverage vehicle, and yes, I'm going to talk about one right now.

It's called [ACME Corporation]. ACME Corporation is a big company did a kazillion dollars in sales last year, and yet, there's a good chance you've never heard of ACME Corporation, or if you have, you don't really know what they do.

But you will.

Worldwide News Magazine *recently featured ACME Corporation on the front page of their "Amazing Companies" section as one of the top 3 performing companies over the last ten years.* The Wall Street Journal *recently featured ACME Corporation as one of the Top 100 Best Companies in America. And* Big Bucks Management Company, *one of the leading investment firms in the world, just added ACME to their list of the top 100 companies in the universe, alongside household names like Amalgamated Dust, Ball-Mart, Persimmon Products and Killer-Diller Industries.*

The bottom line is that ACME is a company with a solid background and a proven sales history and yet, they are just getting started.

Right now, over a million individuals and businesses own one or more ACME products, and that's a big number, but the market for ACME products is estimated to be over 100 million. Noted expert, Casper D. Ghost said: "it's only a matter of time before everyone owns an ACME product."

So what kinds of products does ACME offer? State-of-the-art explosives, traps, slings, catapults, cages, boulders, and other devices for capturing road runners in large quantities. According to Wile E. Coyote, *a noted expert and ACME customer, ACME's products are best in class.*

ACME products make roadrunner catching easier and less time-consuming. They allow you to capture more roadrunners in less time and at a much lower cost. In fact, some ACME products allow you to set up automated road runner devices that work for you while you're at lunch or at work or doing anything else.

ACME has products that everyone needs, and will always need. In good times and bad, people will always have road runners to catch and no other company offers what ACME offers. That's why ACME's future is so incredibly solid.

Because the market for ACME products is so big, there is a big financial opportunity for you. The question is, how do you leverage this to achieve wealth and time freedom. What exactly will you be doing?

The answer is simple. You talk to people about the ACME BUSINESS and about the ACME PRODUCTS and if you're too busy to do that, then you use marketing tools that have been created for you like websites, like a voicemail presentation such as this one, like live conference calls, and other tools. You get people to access these tools like you're doing right now, and somebody else does the talking for you.

When someone buys one of our products, you get paid, and when someone gets started in the business and they sign up somebody who buys an ACME product, you get paid on that, too.

You get paid not just on your efforts but on the efforts of other people and as more and more people get started, you get the power of numbers working for you—it's called leverage and it creates tremendous wealth.

Last year, every 12 days, ACME Corporation recognized a new hundred-thousand dollar income-earner, and every 26 days, they recognized a new two-hundred and fifty-thousand dollar income earner. Thousands of people are earning a thousand dollars per month in extra income, part-time, with ACME Corporation. Hundreds of people are earning $5,000 per month. And more than a dozen people are earning a million dollars a year with ACME Corporation.

Now you don't have to quit your job or current occupation to do this and there's absolutely no capital risk whatsoever. You can start part-time—a few hours a week—you can do this from the comfort of your home, and there's no limit to the amount you can earn or how quickly you can earn it.

ACME Corporation is attracting people from all walks of life, people who have never been in business before and want to earn some extra income, corporate executives, business owners, real estate brokers, professional athletes, medical doctors, and attorneys, like me, looking for time freedom and retirement income. I no longer practice law because ACME Corporation has the greatest business opportunity I've ever seen and I'm not going to miss out. Neither should you.

I want you to remember today's date. Look at your calendar. Where you are in life, today is a direct result of the decisions you made five years ago and where you're going to be five years from now will be the result of the decisions you make today.

Right now, you have an important decision to make. You can either hang up the phone and continue doing what you're doing, or you can get started with us. Get back to the person who gave you this number and tell them you want to get started with ACME Or tell them you have some questions or want more information, but don't miss out on this opportunity to create financial freedom and time freedom and an incredible lifestyle so many of us now enjoy.

Thanks again for listening.

SCRIPT: IMAGINE HOW YOU WILL FEEL

This is the transcript of a live recruiting conference call I did. The original was approximately 20 minutes long and included live testimonials from four distributors. Sizzle calls aren't usually this long (and don't include live testimonials) but our team was getting good results with the call and we started using the replay as a sizzle call

If you cut out the live testimonials and edit out a lot of the details about the product and company, you could get this down to under ten minutes.

Unlike the previous script, I have not included language about a fictitious company and products. Instead, I have prompted you to insert that information about your own company and products.

Also note, unless you promote this as "the replay of a recent live conference call," which you could do, you'll want to omit references to the time of day, e.g., "Good Evening" and "Tonight".

LIVE RECRUITING CALL CONVERTED TO SIZZLE CALL

Good Evening, this is David Ward calling in from Orange County, Califor-

nia.I want to welcome you and thank you for taking the time to call. In the next few minutes, we're going to be talking about making money. I don't know where you are in life right now but many people I talk to these days tell me they need more income. Tonight, we're going to show you how you can earn hundreds or even thousands of dollars a month in extra income, part-time, from the comfort of your own home and you'll hear from a few people, just like you, who are doing exactly that.

I'm going to tell you about a company I found out about around [number] years ago. At the time, I was an attorney in private practice and for over twenty years I earned a very good living but, as you might expect, I was always working and didn't have enough time to do the things that are really important like spending time with my family.

And so when I found out about this company and what they offered, I got excited because they don't just offer the opportunity for extra income, they also offer the potential for residual income which meant I could create financial freedom and time freedom and boy that really appealed to me.

I got started and even though I was extremely busy, I managed to put a few hours a week into my new business. In a few months, I was earning thousands of dollars a month in extra income, and in a few years, I had replaced the six-figure income from my law practice with a six-figure residual income. Today, I'm retired from the practice of law, I work from home, I get to help people every day, and I have lots of free time.

Now, let me tell you a little about the company that made all this possible.

The name of our company is [company name] and what we do is simple: [what your company does, what they offer, why it is valuable]

[Details about the need for your products or services/size of the market; one to three sentences]

[More information about what the products/services do, how they work, how customers benefit]

Imagine how you'll feel knowing. . . [features/benefits customers get from your product or service]

Not only that. . . [additional features and benefits]

But I'm not done. You also get. . . [another important feature/big benefit]

So, what does all this cost? Believe it or not, it's only. . . [price]

Alright, let's talk about how you make money with [company name]. What exactly will you be doing?

Well, you talk to people about the business and about the products and we have marketing tools that make this easy to do, like websites, voicemail presentations, live conference calls such as this one, DVDs, and online videos. . . You simply get people to access these tools, like you're doing right now, and somebody else does the talking for you.

When someone buys [product/service], you get paid [amount/range], and when someone gets started in the business and they sign somebody up, you get paid a percentage of that, too. You get paid not just on your efforts but on the efforts of other people and as more and more people get started, you get the power of numbers working for you—it's called leverage and it creates tremendous wealth.

[Details about distributors having success/reaching income milestones] And there's plenty more ahead.

What do I mean? [More details about the size of the market/need for the products, quotes from experts about why people need and buy what we offer. . .]

And that means there's a huge financial opportunity for you with [company name].

We have people from all walks of life, all ages, all backgrounds, most working spare time and bringing in an extra $500, $1000, $2,000 a month, with [company], most of them with no prior experience in business. We have stay at home moms, young people looking for an alternative to a corporate job, school teachers, blue-collar workers, and we also have real estate and mortgage professionals, salespeople, corporate executives, medical doctors, and other professionals looking for a Plan B.

I've invited a few people on the call tonight, some part-time, some full-time, to share with you their experience with our company:

Let's go out to. . . [testimonial number one]

Next, let's go out to. . . [testimonial number two]

The next individual is. . . [third testimonial]

Last but not least, we're going to hear from [fourth testimonial]

Wow, great stories. As you can see, anyone can be successful in this business and that's because we have a simple, step-by-step system that anyone can follow. We have training calls and websites that show you what to do and how to do it and a team of people who will help you get started and work with you to help you build your business. You don't need experience or talent to earn income with [company], just the desire to get ahead and the willingness to put in some time and effort.

Now, you're probably thinking, "this sounds good, but it sounds expensive" In the US, a small franchise that doesn't offer the income potential of [company] might require you to invest $15 or $20 thousand dollars, or more, to start your business, but you can start your own [company] business for a onetime investment of just [amount]. [Amount] to start a business that could pay you a fortune. But I have more good news—right now, [details about a promotion we had that month].

GET BACK with the person who invited you on the call and tell them you want to get started with [company]. Don't miss this opportunity to create financial freedom and time freedom and an incredible lifestyle so many of us now enjoy. I look forward to hearing about your success! Thanks again for dialing in.

SCRIPT: YOUR ONLY OPTION

This script tells prospects why they need to start their own business.

SAMPLE SCRIPT—YOUR ONLY OPTION

Hello and thanks for calling. If you're like most people, this message might tick you off. And you know what? That's exactly what it should do. If things aren't going the way you want them to right now, if you're not happy with your income or your job or if you're up to your eyeballs in debt or struggling to pay your bills, if you're concerned about your family's future, you need to get angry and then you need to DO something about it.

Here's the truth: you can't hope and pray for things to get better, you've got to MAKE them better. If you want to earn more income, pay your bills, get out of debt, well hey, this isn't a movie with a guaranteed happy ending, its real life and if you want things to change, YOU have to change.

So, what are your options?

As far as I'm concerned, there's really only one option. But before I tell you what it is, let me tell you who I am.

My name is Jim Anderson. I own a successful business I run from home. Before that, I worked in the tech industry. I had some good years but a few years ago, I was laid off. I looked for another job but you know how it is, nobody wants to hire someone with a lot of experience when they can hire someone younger for half the pay.

I kept looking but nobody was hiring and I didn't know what to do. When my unemployment and savings ran out, I started using my credit cards to pay my bills and things just got worse.

I know what it's like when the bills are piling up and you're borrowing on Mastercard to pay Visa and Visa to pay American Express. I know what it's like to eat peanut butter and jelly sandwiches or popcorn for dinner. I know what it's like to be stressed out all the time, unable to sleep because you're worried about . . . EVERYTHING.

I thought about starting a business but I had no idea what to do. Most people say they want to start a business but most people never do it. Why is that?

The first reason: money; they don't have tens of thousands, or hundreds of thousands of dollars set aside to buy or start a business. I sure didn't have that kind of money after I was laid off.

Reason number two: risk; if you put your life savings into a business and you lose it, what then? A lot of people don't want to take that chance.

The third reason: they don't have the time; they're working long hours at their job and barely have time to catch some sleep before they have to do it all over again the following day.

The fourth reason most people don't start a business even though they'd like to is that they simply don't know what to do. Most businesses require some expertise, some experience; if you've never run a business before, how can you expect to be successful? It's crazy, right?

And yet, starting a business is the only option.

I got lucky. One day, I met a guy who told me his story. He said he'd always wanted to start a business but didn't have much money or any idea what to do. I could certainly relate to that. He said he finally found a business he could start at home, with no previous business experience. He said there was plenty of training and help available and so he got started part time. Well, one thing led to another, and that business was now his primary source of income.

He asked me if I'd like some information. I said sure, I'd take a look. Wouldn't you?

He sent me the information, and I really liked what I saw. In fact, everything made sense. I asked a lot of questions and then, I got started.

Within a few months, my new part-time business was paying me several thousand dollars a month. Within a few years, I was earning a six-figure income. Today, I work from home, I love what I do, and I have lots of free time. I'll never need to look for a job again.

Now, you're probably wondering what we do, am I right? Let me tell you. . .

[Add information about products or services, company, and compensation]

Look, I don't know you and I don't know if this would be right for you but I do know it's worth taking a look. If you're ready to make some changes in your life, I suggest you take a chance and look at the information. It won't cost you anything to look.

When I met that guy a few years ago, I never imagined it would be the start of an amazing new chapter in my life. But it was and it could be for you too.

Get back to the person who asked you to listen to this message. Tell them you want to get started, or tell them you want more information, but don't let this opportunity pass you by. Thanks for listening.

SCRIPT: RECRUITING PROFESSIONALS— GENERAL

If you're read my book, *Recruiting Up*, you know that in my business, I've recruited a lot of professionals. Here is a script for a sizzle call I've used.

SAMPLE SCRIPT FOR RECRUITING PROFESSIONALS

Hello and thanks for listening. If you're a professional or own your own business and you're looking for an additional source of income, I think you're going to like this message.

My name is David Ward and I'm an attorney in Southern California. I'm retired now after practicing for more than twenty years and people always ask me why I walked away from a successful law practice. It's simple. Although I earned a great living as a lawyer, I had no free time. I was always at the office or in court or stuck in traffic and I was starting to burn out.

I made too much money to quit but not enough to retire, so I started looking for a Plan B, something I could do part time that would be appropriate for a professional.

One day a friend asked me if I had heard about a company called [company name]. They offer [one sentence about the primary product].

[Describe what you like about your company's product, product line, or mission.]

I checked out the company, and I liked what I saw. They have an excellent reputation. I found out that I could get paid for referring people to their [product] so I signed up as a distributor and began telling everyone I knew about the [products] and the business opportunity. I did this a few hours a week and within a few months, I was earning several thousand dollars per month in extra income. In a few years, I had replaced the six-figure income from my law practice with a six-figure income with [company].

But here's the thing. My [company] income is passive income. It comes in month after month, year after year, whether I'm working, traveling, or doing nothing at all. I now have time freedom and retirement income, and I accomplished this in just a few years.

I'm not alone. Thousands of people earn passive income with [company]. Hundreds of distributors earn six-figure incomes and some earn seven-figures.

Well now that I've got your attention, you're probably wondering how you can participate.

There are three options.

The first option is to offer [company products] to your clients and contacts. This can be as simple as sending people to your [company] website to watch some videos. When someone signs up for a [product], you get paid. If they buy a [a bigger package] you get paid even more.

Not only do you get paid when someone signs up, you get paid again every time they [re-order]. You can sign up someone one time and get paid over and over again for the next five or ten or twenty years, earning true residual income. I'm still getting paid on [products] I sold more than [number] years ago.

The second option is [retailing products to businesses, groups, etc.] Many [company] distributors earn six-figure incomes marketing [company] products. If you have a sales background or you want to generate a full time income right away, this could be a great choice.

The third option is to sign up other distributors. When they sell [products], you get paid a percentage. I've signed up real estate and insurance professionals, business owners, doctors, lawyers, friends and family, and you can, too. Who do you know who might be interested in earning more income or starting a new career? They can sign up others, too, and you'll be paid a percentage on that business, as well.

You can choose any of these options, or all of them. When I got started with [company], I focused on option three. I showed my friends and business contacts what I was doing and signed up a lot of people who wanted to do the same thing. They signed up other distributors, and as my network grew, so did my income. Today, I get paid from the efforts of thousands of people.

Besides the money, what I like best about [company] is that it allows me to help a lot of people and let's face it, today, there are a lot of people who need help with [the types of problems our products address]. There are also a lot of people who want to start a business and earn more income and we can help them do that, too.

The market for [company] products? Well, it's huge. Right now, [some stats/sales numbers], and we're just getting started. I no longer practice law because [company] has the greatest income opportunity I've ever seen and I'm not going to miss out and neither should you.

Get back to the person who invited you to listen to this message and tell them you want to get started with [company], or tell them you have some questions or want more information, but don't miss out on this opportunity to create financial freedom and time freedom and an incredible lifestyle so many of us now enjoy. Thanks again for listening.

SCRIPT: RECRUITING REAL ESTATE PROFESSIONALS

This is a different style of script for recruiting real estate professionals. You can modify it to recruit other professionals, business owners, or leaders in other niche markets. Note, this could also be converted to a lead generation message.

SCRIPT FOR RECRUITING REAL ESTATE PROFESSIONALS

Hello and thanks for listening. If you're a real estate or mortgage professional, I think you're going to like this message. In the next few minutes, you're going to hear about something that could literally triple your income in the next twelve months.

My name is David Ward and I'm a retired attorney. I've also been a licensed real estate broker, an investor, and a partner in a real estate seminar company. Today, I own a business that works closely with the real estate community. We help agents and brokers get more clients and increase their income. I'll tell you more about that in a minute.

I practiced law for over twenty years and in some ways, my practice was like the real estate business. I'd work on a case and if it settled, I'd earn a nice fee, and if it didn't, I earned nothing. And every time I closed a file, I'd look at the place in my file drawer where it had been and realize I needed to replace it. In other words, I was only as good as my last client and I was continually looking for new ones.

Don't get me wrong, I earned a very good living as an attorney. I enjoyed a multiple six-figure income, but because of overhead and living expenses and taxes, even after twenty years, I hadn't saved enough to be able to retire. And that's why I started the business I'm in now. It has become my "Plan B" and it could become yours.

Here's what it's all about.

[DETAILS—For or five paragraphs about the problems you address and details about your solutions.]

So let me cut to the chase. Our company is expanding nationwide and we need help. We're not offering you a job, we're not looking for investors, what we need is you. Your contacts, your skills, and your desire to earn a lot of money helping us bring our services to the market.

You can do this part time or full time. It won't interfere with your real estate career in any way; in fact, it will actually enhance it by allowing you to generate more leads and more referrals.

You can earn an extra $2,000 to $10,000 a month, in addition to your real estate income. If you're good, you could earn a lot more than that, yes, even tripling your current income.

The best part is that we also offer you a way to create residual income. Residual income is like selling a property once and getting paid a commission every year the buyer owns the property. Think about that for a minute.

Residual income is the reason I started this business. In a few short years, I was able to create a six-figure passive, residual income. The money comes in month after month, year after year, whether I'm working or on vacation or doing nothing at all. Now I have time freedom. I can do what I want when I want and never have to think about money again. And of course I now have the retirement income I never had before.

Hundreds of people have been able to generate a six-figure residual income with our company and you can, too. One of my partners walked away from a six-figure real income with his family-owned real estate business; he now earns a seven-figure residual income with our company.

I realize that what we do may not be for you. And that's okay. We're not looking for everyone. But if you'd like more information about what we do and how you can partner with us, please get back to the person who sent you here. They'll get you complete information with no cost or obligation so you can make an informed decision.

Take care and thanks again for listening.

CHAPTER 4: THE EASY WAY TO WRITE A SIZZLE CALL SCRIPT

The easiest way to create a sizzle call script is to record and transcribe existing sizzle calls and live conference calls used by other distributors in your company. You could also record live business overviews presented in your local market, or record yourself or another distributor doing a sit-down presentation.

Transcripts of these messages and presentations should provide you with most of the material you will need for your script.

If you want more, sit down with a recorder and pretend you're talking to a prospect, telling them about the products and business and why they should sign up. Or record someone else doing that.

Go through the company literature, websites, videos, and other tools, and write down key points you may want to include in your script.

Finally, as you go through your notes, think about stories you can share to illustrate the benefits you will present in your message. One or two product stories and one or two business stories should be enough.

OUTLINING YOUR SCRIPT

A recruiting sizzle call should include the following elements:

1. **Opening/Welcome.** Introduce yourself. Tell your story. Tell callers why they should listen to the message.
2. **Frame the problem.** Describe or acknowledge the problem(s) the caller is likely to have that your products/business can help resolve.
3. **Agitate the problem.** How bad could it get? What might happen if they do nothing, or they wait too long?
4. **Present the solution.** What can your products and business do to solve their problem or help them achieve a goal? Tell them the features (what it is, how it is made). Tell them the benefits (what it can do for them). Offer proof. Answer FAQs and/or overcome common objections.
5. **Call to action.** Tell them what to do next, e.g., sign up for the business, ask for more information, etc.

Let's look at each of these elements.

1. OPENING/WELCOME

Your first few sentences are critical to getting prospects to focus. If you have a good opening, prospects will continue to listen. If you don't, they may tune out or hang up.

You can greet them, as I usually do in my scripts, but make it brief. You want them to know, as quickly as possible, that what they are about to hear is something that will benefit them. Tell them why they should listen, what they will learn, or how they will be better off.

One way to open the message is to ask a question or a series of questions about the prospect's current situation, a problem they want to solve, or their desire to improve some aspect of their life.

Here's an example:

"Are you interested in earning more income? If so, I think you're going to like this message. In the next few minutes, you're going to learn about a

simple way to start a part-time, home-based business. You don't need a lot of time, you don't need a lot of money, and you don't need any business experience. Let me tell you what this is all about."

Another way to open your message is to make a bold statement that hints at a benefit and makes prospects curious to hear more. If you offer a weight loss product, for example, you might open with something like this:

"I lost 30 pounds in 90 days, without diet or exercise and I've kept the weight off for the last six months. If you want to lose weight and keep it off, without diet or exercise, keep listening. In the next 3 minutes, I'm going to tell you how I did it, and how you can, too."

Follow this by introducing yourself and telling your story.

Some sizzle calls use an anonymous speaker, someone who doesn't provide their name or tell their story. They are merely a narrator, delivering what amounts to a commercial. This can work but there are advantages to introducing yourself and telling your story. Prospects can see you are a real person. They can relate to you and your "struggle". In hearing how you solved a problem or achieved a goal, they can see what's possible for them.

You don't have to tell your entire story at the beginning of the call. In the beginning, you might mention your background and what brought you to the products or business, tell the rest of your story (e.g., your results, progress) later in the message.

Unless the call is specifically targeted at network marketers, I suggest you avoid using network marketing terminology—titles, rank, upline/downline, etc. You don't want to confuse people about what those terms mean, or put too much emphasis on the network marketing aspects of the business before callers are ready to hear that. Instead, use terms everyone can understand: "Leader in our company, reached the top position, one of my business partners, one of my mentors, built a big business (instead of a big team)".

Most people have a very short attention span today. Many prospects are only half-listening to your message. They're easily distracted by the TV, their kids, other calls or texts. Just as you have to work to get their attention at the beginning of the message, you have to work to keep it.

One way to do that is to talk to them directly, as though they are the only person on the call. Avoid saying things like, "Everyone dialing in," "All of you," or asking, "Have any of you. . ."; instead, say "YOU":

- Have you ever. . ?
- When was the last time you. . ?
- How much is that costing you?
- I'm sure you've tried. . . ., am I right?
- Will you ever be able to. . ?
- I want to ask you a question. . .

Another way to keep people listening is to "salt" the message with glimpses of what lies ahead. You can see that in the weight loss opening above where it says, ". . .keep listening. I'm going to tell you how I did it, and how you can, too."

You can do this anywhere in your message. Before you get to the compensation, for example, you might say, "I'm going to tell you how we earn money in this business, and how you can earn $1,000 or more in your first week. But first, I need to tell you about. . ."

Another way to do it is to tell callers something they will hear at the end of the call—a special offer or some other incentive to listen to the entire message.

(2) FRAME THE PROBLEM

Before you present your products or business (your solution) you need to talk about the problem(s) callers are likely to have. If the prospect doesn't know about issues in their drinking water, for example, they won't appreciate what your water purification system can do for them.

One of the simplest ways to frame a problem is to get the prospect to acknowledge (to themselves) that they have the problem or that they fear they will get it. Asking questions is the easiest way to do that.

Do you want to lose weight? Lower your blood pressure? Look younger and feel better?

Are you saving enough for retirement? For your kid's college? To buy a home?

Do you want to earn more income? Work for yourself? Work from home?

Your may earn a great income on your job but let me ask you, how much do you earn when you don't work?

In answering questions like these, prospects are admitting they have a problem or something they want to obtain.

Another way to frame the problem is to incorporate it into your story. When I talk about why I started my business—my frustration with working long hours, my lack of options for retirement, and so on—many prospects relate to my story, and me, because they are in the same boat. If your story doesn't lend itself to this, you can tell them about customers or distributors who had those problems or desires.

You know what? Go ahead and tell them my story. "I know this lawyer who. . ."

You can also frame the problem by quoting experts or authorities, or by citing statistics. For example, you might quote an article you read describing how many people are struggling with too much debt.

(3) AGITATE THE PROBLEM

Once you've stated the problem, instead of immediately presenting the solution, show prospects that the problem probably won't go away by itself and that it may actually get worse.

The prospect is overweight, their credit card balances are too high, they want to earn more money, they want to be able to retire, and so on. Agitating these problems means tapping into the emotions prospects are likely to feel about those problems and their inability to solve them.

An overweight prospect usually knows she is overweight. But that doesn't mean she is ready to do something about it. To get her to take action, buy your products, for example, you need to make her feel something that compels her to act.

If you quote a physician stating how obesity can shorten lifespan, for example, or a story about a relative of yours who passed away at an early age, the prospect may think about how she might live long enough to see her kids or grandkids get married.

People buy based on emotions. You need to supply facts to prove you can deliver the results they want, but it is their feelings or emotions that gets them to take action.

You can also talk about what you (or others) have tried in the past that didn't work out.

When I talk about looking for a Plan B so I could build retirement income, I often mention that the other businesses I looked at "were either too expensive, too time-consuming, or just plain silly". I talk about being frustrated and close to giving up. Anyone who has looked at business opportunities and been frustrated by what they saw will remember how they felt.

(4) PRESENT THE SOLUTION—PRODUCT INFO

Once you've framed the problem, and agitated it, tell prospects about your solutions. Tell them what your products or services do to solve those problems.

Here is the types of product information you should consider covering:

- Features (what it is, what it does)
- Benefits (what customers get, how they are better off)
- Advantages/how it compares to competition/how it compares to doing nothing
- Patents/awards/unique features
- Cost/value/purchase options
- Special offers/money back guarantee
- Success stories/testimonials/reviews/awards

Prospects want to know what you sell, the benefits customers get, and why your products are better than your competition. They want to know that the products are safe and effective and hear about people who are using them and seeing results. If your products cost more than the competition, they want you to tell them why they are worth more.

You won't be able to tell everything, of course. Tell them a few key points about your products or services. What stood out for you when you first heard about your company's products?

COMPANY/MARKET

At some point, you should say a few things about the company. Not a lot. There isn't time for that, nor do prospects want to know a lot at this point. Give them a few highlights, to build trust, to show the company's position in the marketplace and the bright future that lies ahead.

Here are some items to consider:

- The company's mission or story
- The company's "USP" (Unique Selling Proposition")—what makes it different or better
- Sales/revenue/profits
- Length of time in business; **not new** (history of success), or **new** (get in before it takes off)

- Public or private company and what that means to distributors
- Ownership/management team experience
- Product or service line(s)
- States/countries open for business; plans for the future
- Accolades/awards/ratings/ reviews/
- Proprietary products or systems/other trust factors
- Market size/competition/growth history/projections

BUSINESS/COMPENSATION

Your message needs to show prospects a picture of what distributors do, convince them that they can do it and that it will be worth it. Talk to them about:

- What distributors do to retail and recruit
- Compensation (commissions, overrides, bonuses) and how much they can earn
- How much time they will have to put in
- What it takes to get their first check/promotion
- Training and support/tools and systems
- Lead/advertising program
- Success stories, especially of distributors from similar backgrounds/situations
- Can they work from home? What do they need (e.g., computer, tablet, smart-phone)?
- What it takes to get started (time, money); ongoing costs
- What they need to do to "break even" (earn back their start-up costs)

Tell them the facts and tell them stories about distributors who have accomplished their goals or are in the process of doing that. Show prospects that they can be successful in the business by following the systems already in place.

You should also address frequently asked questions and common objections. For example, since most prospects have never owned a business, you should tell them that previous business experience isn't necessary, and why (e.g., training, systems, support, tools, etc.)

See my book, *Recruit and Grow Rich,* for a detailed discussion of common network marketing objections and how to overcome them.

(5) CALL TO ACTION

A sizzle call is basically a sales letter delivered verbally. The objective is to "sell" the prospect on getting started in your business and/or buying your products, or at least taking the next step to learn more.

Although it is unlikely that you will sign up prospects solely on the basis of a sizzle call, it does happen. Therefore, you should always "assume the sale". Tell prospects how to get started in the business (and/or buy something) and encourage them to do that:

- "Get back to the person who invited you to this message and tell them you want to get started with [company]. Or tell them you want more information. If you have any questions, they'll make sure you get them answered. . ."
- "Get back to the person who invited you to this message and ask them to tell you about the next event [or live conference call] in your area"
- "Get back to the person who invited you to listen to this message and ask them for the link to their [company/distributor] website so you can get started/learn more. . ."
- "Get back to the person who invited you to this call and ask them to show you. . . [e.g., how you can earn $1000 in the next ten days. . .]"

WHAT TO LEAVE OUT

You won't use all the above elements in a sizzle call. Remember, you're showing prospects the sizzle, not the steak, veggies, or dessert.

Leave out most of the details of the comp plan. Most people aren't able to follow everything anyway, especially over the phone. Mention that the company pays commissions, overrides, and bonuses, and tell them what it takes to get their first commission and their first override. You can also give them one or two examples of what it takes to achieve a certain income level. (Again, make sure you abide by the law and company policy regarding income claims.)

You won't have time to talk about your entire product line. Choose one or two signature products to talk about. You can mention others but focus on one or two.

Don't "date" your message. Avoid saying anything about the weather, the holidays, or anything else that would make your message sound "out of date" to someone hearing it six months later.

Your sizzle message should focus on the basics a prospect wants to know: what you do (your products), how much they can earn, and what they will need to do to earn it.

Your job is to give them enough information, but not too much. A few examples, but not too many. Show them what you do and get them excited about joining you.

Many sizzle calls begin by talking about a problem or desire and how the presenter (or someone they know) discovered the product. They talk about how the product helped them and how they began telling others about that product. Then they talk about the company and the business.

There is a natural flow to this, and it's a good model to follow.

I also lead with my story, but it is centered on the business, not the product. I talk about how I wanted to work fewer hours and build retirement income and describe how I found the business opportunity. Then I talk about the company and the product and come back to the business (income and lifestyle) before I close.

How long should the message be? Many sizzle calls are between 2 and 5 minutes. Mine are usually longer, seven or eight minutes. What can I tell you, lawyers talk a lot.

Some messages are even longer—10, 15, even 20 or 25 minutes. Technically, these aren't sizzle calls and many "experts" will tell you this is impossibly long. They say you can't have a message longer than a few minutes or you'll lose people. I say you can't have a BAD message or you'll lose people. If you have a good message, and you have an interested prospect, they will listen all the way to the end and get excited about hearing more.

People read 300-page books. They listen to two-hour presentations. If your message is well done, if it presents the information in an effective and compelling way, and if the prospect needs or wants what you offer, they will listen to a longer message.

If you're going to record a longer message, however, I suggest you also record a shorter message you can use as a sorting tool. See Chapter 7 regarding how I use sizzle calls to sort and do exposures.

SPECIALTY MESSAGES

I mentioned earlier that one of the reasons for setting up your own sizzle calls is that you can record messages that target different niches. Specialty messages can use terminology, examples, and stories tailored to the niche market.

Attorneys who hear my sizzle call for attorneys relate to me and my story. They know that I'm "one of them," and if I can succeed in this network marketing business, they can, too. If you have sizzle call for real estate agents, have a real estate agent on your team record it and tell their story. Have them talk about issues in the industry and share stories about other agents who are joining the team.

Specialized calls also allow you to hit the right hot buttons for the niche market. Professionals, for example, tend to earn a lot of income but often sacrifice time with their family or have health issues due to working long hours under stressful conditions.

A message targeted to college students or recent college graduates would talk about the job market and the advantages of starting a business instead of depending on a corporate job.

A message for people who are retired or retiring soon would talk about supplemental income. It would also address the fear many seniors have of running out of savings and having to look for a job and compete with younger workers.

A message for people in the creative arts—actors, artists, writers, musicians, and so on—would have the speaker talk about how they love what they do but they needed a source of income to be able to do it, and how they found that when they started their business with your company.

A message directed to prospects with network marketing experience would use network marketing lingo and talk about the issues that many distributors encounter: getting leads, comp plan issues, company integrity, upline support, training, and so on.

A message for recruiting doctors might feature a physician on your team speaking about the massive overhead of running a medical practice today, and how this limits his ability to provide quality care to patients. He might then talk about how he earns as much income as a distributor with almost no overhead.

As your team grows, you should consider creating additional sizzle call messages (and lead capture messages) to target niche markets.

You can also create other types of recorded messages:

- Testimonials. A message featuring 10 or 15 (or more) successful distributors telling their 30-second story. This can be used as a "closing" tool or a regular exposure tool. I've seen messages like this successfully used as a first or second exposure. (Again, make sure you follow the law and company policy regarding monetary claims.)

- Comp plan: A detailed explanation of how the comp plan works, for prospects who want to know the details.
- Company credibility. Some prospects may want to know more about your company's history, patents, processes, awards, market share, prospects for the future, and so on.
- Getting started training. Tell new distributors what to do first and also, what NOT to do. Tell them what to put on their calendar. Tell them which tools your team recommends and where to get training. A getting started message might also be used as a recruiting tool, to show prospects what they will do when they sign up.
- Product details. Specifics about how your products are manufactured, what's in them, why they are unique or better than what other companies offer, etc.
- A "new product" message. When your company introduces a new product or service, you can record a call that tells prospects everything they need to know. You could also do a training message for distributors, about how to introduce the new product to customers.
- A "coming soon" message. When your company is about to open in a new country, you can record a call that tells existing and prospective distributors what's coming and what to do to get ready for it.

The more you use recorded messages, the more ways you'll find to use them.

PART III

RECORDING AND PROMOTING YOUR MESSAGES

Once you have written a script and you're ready to record your first message, the next step is to set up an account with a voicemail service. Chapter 5 shows you the company I use and recommend. You can set up a new account in a few minutes.

Chapter 5 also provides tips on recording your message.

Chapter 6 shows you how to promote your lead capture message so you can start getting leads.

Chapter 7 shows you how to use your new sizzle call (or any sizzle call) to do exposures.

CHAPTER 5: HOW TO GET A FREE VOICEMAIL ACCOUNT AND RECORD YOUR MESSAGES

Once you have a script for a sizzle call or lead capture message, the next step is to set up an account with a company that provides voice-mail services. There are many companies to choose from, offering different features and different prices. The one I currently use and recommend is SimpleVoiceBox.com. The service is good quality, it's easy to use, and they offer free and low-cost paid options.

With a free line, the caller dials the number assigned to you and is prompted to enter a code (extension) to hear the message. For $5 per month you can get a direct line with no extension. The caller dials the number and, once connected, your message starts playing. Just like voicemail on your phone.

I've used both types and while I prefer the direct line because it's easier to give prospects the number, and easier for them to dial and avoid mis-dialing, I haven't had any issues with the free line and use that too.

As you set up your account, you will be asked to elect a free number, (with an extension), a paid number (no extension) or a toll-free number, which costs extra. Since most people have unlimited long distance on their mobile phones today, you probably don't need a toll-free number.

Next, you'll choose the type of message you want. If you choose "play and record," the system will play your *outgoing* message to callers and when it's done, prompt them to leave a message. If you choose "play only," the system plays your outgoing message and then "hangs up".

For a lead capture line, choose "play and record". For a sizzle call or a similar message, e.g., training, choose "play only". You can change this setting at any time.

The next step is to record your outgoing message. You can do this over the phone (by dialing your assigned number and following the voice prompts to record) or by recording elsewhere—on your phone, on your computer, etc.—and uploading the message file. I'll discuss these options later.

Finally, you will be asked if you want to receive a call log. This is a list of the phone numbers of all callers, the time they called, how long they listened to the outgoing message, and if they left a message (if the account is set to "play and record"). The log will be sent to you daily via email.

A call log is valuable information for both sizzle calls and lead capture messages. For a lead capture line, you'll also want to listen to the messages left by prospects which you can do by calling your number and entering a code, or you by logging into your account online.

You can set up an account at SimpleVoiceBox.com and start using it as soon as you've recorded an outgoing message. Start with the free option and try it out. If you want to switch to the paid option, (with a direct phone number), you'll be assigned a different phone number and you can move your outgoing message from the free account to the paid account.

Note that the company has the right to change the telephone number they assign to you. I've had it happen once or twice over the years. You may use a number for six months or six years and suddenly find that that number is no longer available. The company provides you with several months notice before they make the switch, but it can be inconvenient, especially if you do a lot of advertising.

If you are concerned about this, you might take a look at other companies. I've used American voicemail (http://americanvoicemail.com/mlm-voicmail/) and also recommend them. They've been around a long time and serve many network marketing companies and teams. They can handle high volume calling, which may be important to you if do a lot of advertising, but they don't offer a free or low cost option.

American voicemail (and other companies) offer other options you may want to use. For example, you may want the caller to hear a menu they can choose from to hear different messages, e.g., "press 1 to hear about our products, "press 2 to hear about our opportunity," etc.

RECORDING YOUR MESSAGE

Recording a lead capture message is simple. If you've ever recorded a voicemail message on an answering machine or on your phone, you already know what to do. Your outgoing message doesn't have to be perfect. Mistakes, uhs, and other verbal "typos" are okay and may actually improve the message by showing listeners it was recorded by a real person.

If you have a very heavy accent, however, or another reason for not wanting to record the message, ask someone on your team or in your upline to do it for you. But try to avoid this. You want callers to hear your name and voice and your story so that when you follow-up with them, they recognize you and are more likely to answer their phone or call you back.

If you have someone else record the message, you'll need to modify your script to omit your name and story since someone else will be speaking. Another option is to have the other person use *their* name and story. When you contact the leads, you can tell them they left a message for your business partner and you're following up on their behalf.

A sizzle call is longer and requires more practice to deliver effectively. Although there are advantages to recording it yourself in terms of leadership for your team, if you don't feel up to the task, ask an experienced presenter in your upline or on your team to record it.

READING THE SCRIPT

Some people say that when you record the message, you shouldn't read the script because it will sound like you are reading. They say you will sound more natural and conversational if you use bullet points or notes. I disagree. I've done it both ways and recommend reading the script.

Reading the script means you won't leave anything out. You'll be able to deliver all the right words, in the right order, and you won't waste time gathering your thoughts or finding the best way to phrase them. You won't spend too much time on one subject and neglect another.

Time is of the essence on a recorded message. You need to deliver the message quickly, confidently, and with high energy. The best way to do that is by reading a script.

How do you make it sound like you aren't reading? Practice. Lots of practice. And by re-writing the script, if necessary, to make it flow smoothly when you read it.

You probably won't need to do this a lot for a short lead capture message. Practice it a few times, record it, and start using it. You can always re-record it later if you want to.

You'll want to put more time into a sizzle call.

Read the sizzle call script out loud and record yourself. Listen for spots where you hesitate or stumble and put a mark on the page. Rewrite the script to smooth out those areas.

Re-read the script and edit it again until you're comfortable with what you say and how it sounds. Then, read it to someone on your team and get their feedback.

Is anything unclear? Any place where the message drags? Any point that could use a different story or example? Anything you should add, remove, or re-arrange? Ask them to be honest: "Would you use this message with your prospects? Would you promote it to your team?" If they hesitate, ask them to tell you what needs to be improved.

If possible, also read the message to someone who knows nothing about the business. As you do, you will hear the message the way a prospect hears it and this may help you find other things you need to change.

When you're happy with the script and your delivery, record it. You don't need to sound like a professional or a highly polished presenter, nor should you try to. Be yourself. A regular guy or gal who's excited about what you do and wants to share it with others.

If you're still not sure about whether you can do this, my advice is to do it anyway. Give yourself permission to record a "terrible" message. Once you listen to the playback, you may find that it's a lot better than you thought.

Besides, what you think isn't really important. What's important is what other people think, that is, if the message is working. If prospects leave their name at the end of your lead capture message, your message is working. If prospects hear your sizzle call and tell you they want to learn more, your sizzle call is working.

RECORDING TIPS

The simplest way to record a message is to dial the number provided by the voicemail company and follow the audio instructions to record and save your message. Within a few minutes, your message will be "live" and ready to use.

The advantage to doing this is that you don't need any other tools— just your phone. But there are two issues you should be aware of.

First, recordings made over the phone aren't high quality. A poor connection, static on the line, and other reasons may result in a recording that is hard to hear or hard to understand.

The second disadvantage of recording over the phone is that you can't edit the message or improve the sound quality. If you stumbled, mispronounced something, if the call signal strength dropped or the baby in the next room cried, you're either stuck with it or you have to start over.

I've had to re-record calls five or six times in the past and it's not fun. But it's not the end of the world.

The alternative is to record the call on your computer, your smart phone, or on a digital recording device, and upload it. This will allow you to produce a higher quality recording.

You won't get static produced by a phone line. You can use a better microphone. And you can edit and "clean up" the recording before you upload it. Editing the audio file lets you remove coughs, sniffles, echoes and background noises, increase the volume, and otherwise create a cleaner and better sounding recording.

There are many programs available for editing. I use a free, open-source program called Audacity (http://audacityteam.org). It works well but there is a learning curve. There are many videos available online that will teach you what you need to know. But is it worth taking the time to learn how to record and edit audios? To be honest, probably not. I've done recorded messages both ways and I find that it's a better use of my time to practice my script before recording and re-record it if I make a major mistake.

Besides, no matter how good your audio file is, callers will listen to it over the phone and won't be able to hear most of that quality.

So I usually record over the phone.

Here are some tips for producing a better recording:

- If you record over the phone, use a land line if possible, not a mobile phone. Corded or cordless is okay. If you use a headset, make sure it's good quality.
- Do a practice run before you begin. Make sure you know how to use the controls. Record a test message and listen to the playback to make sure you can hear everything.
- Before you start the actual recording, drink a cup of coffee, exercise, or do some deep breathing exercises. Get your energy level up. Drink plenty of water before you begin so you don't have dry mouth. Use the restroom before you start.
- Turn off other devices that make noise or might interrupt you. Tell others in the house not to disturb you.
- Record standing up. It will help you project your voice. Some people like to walk around while recording.
- Smile. People will hear it in your voice.
- Speak naturally, as if you're talking with a friend. In fact, pretend you're speaking to one person, someone you know, just telling them about what you're doing.
- Speak a little more quickly than you usually do. But don't race.
- Speak a little louder than you usually do.
- If you stumble, don't think about it, just keep going. Remember, it doesn't have to be perfect.

Finally, tell yourself that your first recording is "just for practice" and that you can re-record it as many times as you want, or re-record it again at a later time. Because you can.

Relax. Have fun. Get it done.

CHAPTER 6: HOW TO PROMOTE YOUR LEAD CAPTURE MESSAGE

Once you have recorded your lead capture message start promoting it wherever you already promote your business. Put the number (and your headline or offer) in your email signature at the bottom of your outgoing emails. Put it in your social media profiles. Add it to content you publish on your blog or website.

You could put the number on your distributor business cards but I have another suggestion. Order some "generic" business cards that identify you as a consultant or business owner, without identifying your network marketing company by name. That way, when you pass out the cards, prospects won't know what you do, they'll have to **call** your lead capture message to find out.

Use your generic cards when you're networking. When someone asks, "What do you do?" tell them you own a marketing business in the _____ industry, for example, and hand them a card with your recorded message number on it.

When you're out running errands and you see someone you want to approach, start a conversation and ask if they can help you. Tell them you own a business, you're expanding and looking for help. "Do you happen to know anyone who might be interested in earning some extra income, or possibly starting a new career?"

If *they* are interested, they will ask you what kind of work it is or what you do. You could then say, "Oh, do you know someone? Or are you interested yourself?" When they tell you they might be interested (depending on what it is), tell them you're on your way to a meeting (or whatever) and they should call the number on the card to get some information.

TWO OF THE BEST WAYS TO PROMOTE YOUR MESSAGE

There are lots of ways to promote a lead capture message. In this chapter, I'm going to tell you about two methods I've used and recommend.

The first method is called a "voicemail drop" and it's very simple. You call prospects and leave a message on *their* voicemail, directing them to call your lead capture message.

You can do this with purchased leads, directories, or any other list. You can even use it in your warm market.

Let's say you're a mom and you recruit stay-at-home moms. Get a copy of your school's parent directory, call through the list and leave a voicemail message, something like this:

"Hi Judy, my name is Alice Kramden. Our kids go to _____. I got your name out of the parent's directory. The reason for my call is, I run a small business from home and I'm looking for some help. This may seem kind of random but do you happen to know anyone in our area who might be interested in earning some extra income on a very part time basis? I've recorded a message they can call to get some information. If you know someone, or you're interested yourself, call and listen to the message at 444-555-6666. If you have any questions, you can reach me on my cell at 555-343-1111. Thanks, Judy. I appreciate your help."

People are curious and you will get calls. If they like what they hear and want to hear more, they will leave a message (or call you). If they're not interested, you won't hear from them. Nice, huh?

If you're cold calling professionals and business owners, you might leave a message like this one:

"Hi Mr. Jones, this is Barney Rubble. I own a marketing and promotion business in the _____ area. I see you're in the _____ business/industry and I'd like to talk to you about a project I'm working on that could be to our mutual benefit. I don't know if you would have any interest but it could mean a significant source of additional income for you without taking up a lot of your time. I've recorded a short [one minute, etc.] message that provides a quick overview. If you like what you hear and want to learn more, leave a message and I'll call you back. Here's the number for the recorded message: 444-555-6666. If you want to call me, my mobile is 222-444-6600. Talk to you soon."

If you're calling biz opp or network marketing leads, you could leave a regular "call me" message (see Part 4), or a message like this:

"Hi Joe, this is Wally Cleaver. I got your name and number from a company that puts together lists of people looking to start a business/for a way to make money from home. Before we talk, I'd like to show you a little about what we do and how we make money and see if you're at all interested. I've recorded a two-minute message and you can call and listen at any time, 24/7. Here's the number: 999-232-5555. If you like what you hear, leave a message and I'll call you back. If you want to reach me directly, my mobile number is 222-444-6600."

Here's a voicemail drop message you might use in your warm market:

"Hey Trixie, it's Alice. I'm wondering if you could do me a favor. I'm working on a business project [I've started a new business] and I want to get the word out about what I'm doing. I recorded a one-minute message about the business [a product I'm offering] and I'd love to get your feedback. Would you call the number and let me know what you think of the message? The number is 999-888-7777. You can leave your comments at the

end of the recording or just call me on my cell. I really appreciate your help. Talk to you soon".

To get better results with a voicemail drop, consider recording a lead capture message for each niche market you target. If you're calling real estate agents, you would want a message that talks about your background in real estate (or that you work with a lot of people in the real estate industry), and address issues familiar to real estate agents: never having weekends off, always hunting for the next listing, and so on.

If you're calling biz opp leads, your lead capture message might talk about some crazy ideas you've seen or tried, the importance of having products or services that are unique or offer great value, and so on.

The beauty of the voicemail drop is that you can make calls at any time. If the prospect picks up the phone, you can do your regular pitch. If you get their voicemail, go ahead and "drop" your message into theirs.

Many distributors who use the voicemail drop method intentionally call prospects after hours so they won't have to speak with anyone. If you do that, you should be prepared for some surprises.

One time I was cold calling attorneys. I made sure to call late, when nobody was in the office. I was calling the east coast, and it was 2 am their time. I was able to leave a lot of voicemail messages, but then, someone answered the phone!

An attorney was in the office preparing for a trial that began the next morning. He was in no mood to talk to me so I wished him good luck at trial and hung up.

One more thing. With warm market prospects, instead of sending them to your lead capture message you could send them to a sizzle call. You could do the same thing with prospects who called your lead capture line and asked for more information.

You know who these people are and have their contact information.

When you follow up, many of them will have called and listened to the sizzle call and you can find out if they're interested in taking the next step.

PAID ADVERTISING

I mentioned that when I started selling my marketing course to attorneys I ran classified ads in the back of legal magazines and newspapers. Classified ads don't have a lot of room but you don't need a lot of room when you use a recorded message. The ad only has to persuade prospects to call and listen; the recorded message does the rest.

Starting with small ads allows you to test different ads without spending a lot of money. If a small ad doesn't work, you can modify it or stop running it and try something else. If it does work, you can repeat the ad and run it in more publications. That's what I did when my first ads started getting leads. Eventually, I ran bigger "display" ads—one-third page, quarter-page, half-page, even full page. Running bigger ads allowed me to get more leads and lower my overall cost per lead.

I ran my ads in print publications. Today, there are other options. You could start with a small pay-per-click (PPC) ad on Facebook, for example, or through Google Adwords or other platforms. An advantage to pay-per-click ads is that you only pay when someone clicks on your ad. If nobody clicks, you don't pay anything. You can limit the amount you spend for each click and the amount you're willing to spend each day.

If you ads are getting clicks but not enough prospects are calling your message, or you get calls but few messages (leads), you can stop the ad(s) and try something else.

You can also experiment with different keywords and different markets. If you want to target real estate agents or teachers or people who are interested in Internet marketing, you can do that.

Best of all, you can get quick results. You could run your first ad today and start getting calls to your message number within the hour. This means you can quickly find out if your ads are working and start getting leads almost immediately.

If you want to try Facebook ads, go ahead and set up an account. You don't have to "turn on" your ads until you're ready and again, you can pause them at any time.

Don't rule out advertising in print publications, however, especially if you're targeting professionals and other niche markets. You can run highly targeted and highly responsive ads in niche publications, and you can often negotiate the rate you pay. See *Recruiting Up* to learn more about recruiting professionals.

Wherever you advertise, starting with some PPC ads is a good way to try out different ads, (headlines and offers), before you commit to something more expensive or long term.

Take time to learn about the different types of campaigns (e.g., pay-per-click vs. Pay-per-impression, choosing keywords, managing your bids and budget, and testing different elements (copy, offers, graphics). Be prepared to experiment.

Over the last few years, as more people have started using PPC ads, they've become more expensive. So go slowly. Start with a small budget, say $5 per day, and see what happens. If you don't get any clicks, you won't be out anything. If you get clicks but few calls, you won't be out much. If you get clicks and calls, see how many callers leave a message.

You don't have to buy an expensive course to learn how to run a successful pay-per-click campaign. There are lots of books and articles and YouTube videos that will teach you most of what you need to know.

THE CONTENT OF YOUR AD

Your company may supply you with ad copy to use in your lead generation ads. Be careful. Your company means well but their first priority is to protect themselves from problems caused by distributors running misleading ads or ads that violate the law or company policy. As a result, the sample or "approved" ads they provide are often dull and unpersuasive. In addition, these ads often mention the name of the company and/or the products, making them unusable for you.

If your company provides sample ads, look at them for ideas but think twice before running the ads "as is".

What should you do instead? Start by looking at ads being run by other distributors, either in your company or in other companies. Look for ads that appear to be working and use them as a template to create your own. How do you know an ad is working? Well, if you see ads running over and over again, that's usually a good indication that the distributor running them is making money with it.

Don't copy an ad word-for-word. Re-write it, starting with the headline. The headline is, by far, the most important part of any ad, and even more so for classified or small pay-per-click ads. In a few seconds, the headline has to grab the prospect's attention and get them to read the body of the ad.

There are many types of headlines you can use. One of the best is a headline that that promise a benefit.

What do your prospects want or need? What do they want to be, do, or have? Promise this in the headline and you will have their attention.

One of the first ad headlines I ran for my marketing course was: "Attorneys: Get More Clients and Increase Your Income". Attorneys want these benefits, of course, and they were compelled to read the body of the ad where they learned that I was offering a free report.

Another option is to put the offer in your headline. For example: "Free Report Reveals...[what they learn in your report]."

In the body of the ad, say something else about what you are offering.

Elaborate on the benefits or provide a detail or two. As mentioned earlier, in my ad I promised to send them my free report, "How to Get More Clients in a Month Than You Now Get All Year!". This was followed by the call to action: "Call 24-Hours for a Free Recorded Message" and the number.

They called because

- They wanted the information in the report and the report was free.
- The call was free. (It was a toll-free 800 number).
- The message was *recorded*, which meant they didn't have to speak to anyone and they could hang up if they didn't like what they heard. (NOTE: Always tell prospects to call your "recorded message".)
- The message was available "24-hours" which meant they could call at any time, even late at night, instead of waiting until work hours.

WARNING: DON'T RUN ANY AD UNTIL YOU READ THIS!

In crafting your ad, spend most of your time working on the head-line. Again, it is the most important part of *any* ad.

No matter how well your ad is pulling, a different headline might dramatically improve your results. You can't possibly know this, however, until you try different headlines, so try lots of them.

Don't be boring, be bold. Make a big promise. Make people curious. Your ad is competing with other ads for attention and with other elements on the page. You want your ad to stand out.

You might try a "WARNING" headline, for example. Here are some samples:

WARNING: DON'T TAKE ANOTHER NUTRITIONAL SUPPLE-MENT UNTIL YOU LISTEN TO THIS FREE RECORDED MESSAGE!

WARNING: DON'T START A HOME-BASED BUSINESS UNTIL YOU LISTEN TO THIS FREE RECORDED MESSAGE!

WARNING: DON'T START A HOME-BASED BUSINESS UNTIL YOU READ THIS!

WARNING: DON'T SPEND ANOTHER DOLLAR ON [LIFE INSURANCE, MUTUAL FUNDS, BOTTLED WATER, ETC.] UNTIL YOU READ THIS FREE REPORT!

A "Warning" headline is hard to ignore. It makes people curious (and nervous) and implies a benefit, i.e., information that can help them avoid or fix a problem, save money, increase their income, or achieve something important to them.

This type of headline is especially effective for a "community awareness" message. As you may recall that's where you alert prospects to a common problem they may or may not know about but which could have serious consequences if ignored.

HOW DO YOU KNOW YOUR MESSAGE IS WORKING?

You may recall me saying that on the recorded message I used in my publishing business I asked callers to tell me where they saw my ad. If a publication was getting calls and leads, I would continue running ads in that publication. If a publication wasn't producing leads, or enough of them, I would either change the ad or pull out of the publication, at least temporarily.

If you're promoting your message in many places, you could do the same thing. Or, you could wait until you speak to the prospects and ask them.

Another way to track your ads or campaigns is to set up different message lines with different incoming phone numbers or extensions for each of your campaigns.

You'll know if your Facebook ads are working, for example, because the only calls to that phone number will be from your Facebook ads.

If you run multiple Facebook campaigns, with different keywords or targeting different types of prospects, you can set up different numbers for each one.

To determine if an ad and/or message is working, you need to look at your numbers. If you're using SimpleVoiceBox and have requested email reports, you'll receive a daily email for each of your voicemail numbers. The email will tell you:

- How many calls that number received
- The date and time of each call
- The caller's phone number (if available)
- How many minutes the caller listened to your message (rounded up)
- Whether they left a message

When you listen to the messages, you'll also learn:

- The prospect's name
- The phone number they provide, which may be different from the number they called from (on your report)
- Their email address (if you asked for it)
- Additional information you asked them to supply

Listening to their message will also tell you how they "sound". Are they sharp? Excited? Confident? Do they sound like someone you'd like to work with in your business?

Take notes. They'll help you when you contact the prospects.

So. . . how do you know if your message is working?

- If you're getting calls, whatever you're doing to promote the number is working. If you're not getting calls, you need to figure out why. Try different headlines. Re-word the name of the report you offer in your ad. If you don't have an offer, create one. Re-word the "call to action".

- Try different publications. For pay-per-click ads, try different keywords. Target different market segments. If "teachers" isn't producing a sufficient number of calls, perhaps "retired teachers" (if that is available) would do better.
- If you're getting calls but not enough of them, try increasing the amount you pay per click and/or your daily budget.
- If you're getting calls but callers aren't listening to the entire message, re-write your message script and/or work on the delivery of your message. Do you have the right benefits in your message? Are you promising too much? Too little? Are you speaking too slowly? Too quickly?
- If people listen to your entire message but don't leave you a message, you're either targeting the wrong prospects, you're not offering something those prospects want, or they don't believe you. Re-write your message script (or use a different one) and try again.
- If you're getting calls and messages but callers aren't providing all the information you requested, consider re-doing your message and asking for *less* information. If you really don't need a mailing address, for example, don't ask for it. Make it easier for callers to leave a message and you should get more callers doing so.
- If callers aren't leaving their phone number (or they leave a bogus number), as mentioned earlier, consider adding something like this to the end of your message: "No information [product sample, etc.] will be provided without a valid phone number".

THE BOTTOM LINE

When I was advertising for my marketing program, I decided that my message was "working" if 70% or more of the callers left their information requesting my free report. I usually did much better than that but it took a lot of trial and error to get that kind of response. If this is your first time running ads and using voicemail for lead capture, you shouldn't expect results like this right out of the gate.

In fact, you may *never* get that kind of response. The good news is that **you may not need to.**

I say that because while the number of leads and your cost per lead are important, even **more** important is how many of those leads you close.

How many do you recruit? How much do you earn in commissions on their product orders and overrides on their team?

You may not get a lot of calls. You may not get a high percentage of callers leaving a message (for whatever reason). You may spend more per lead than you think you should. But if you're signing up those leads and earning a profit, or you can see that you will do through re-orders and through overrides as your team grows, what you're doing is working.

And *that's* the bottom line.

CHAPTER 7: HOW TO USE SIZZLE CALLS FOR RECRUITING

The network marketing industry has been using sizzle call messages for many years. You may already be using them in your business.

And yet some network marketing leaders don't use sizzle calls. They say that once a prospect has heard your lead generation message, or you have piqued their interest with something you've said (orally or in writing), you should direct them to *a full presentation*. "If you can't tell them everything," they say, "don't tell them anything".

And yet many network marketers use sizzle calls with great success. I'm one of them.

I told you that I use sizzle calls as a sorting tool, to show prospects what I do and quickly find out if they're interested in learning more. I've found that if a prospect doesn't like what they hear on a good sizzle call, *they are unlikely to change their mind by hearing or seeing the full presentation.*

That's if you can get them to see or hear a full presentation. As we know, that's easier said than done.

Have you ever had prospects tell you they will watch your video, visit your website, dial into your conference call, or come to your event, and not do it?

Why do they do that?

They may tell you they will look simply get you off the phone. Or they may intend to do it but it's not important to them and they forget.

They don't look because they **don't know what they don't know.**

They don't know anything about what you offer. How could they? They don't know what's in it for them. So, use a sizzle call to show them.

When you have a prospect listen to a sizzle call as the first step, and they like it, they'll watch your video, etc., because they **want** to. They know something about what you're offering and they are interested.

It's also easier to get a prospect to listen to a five-minute message because you're not asking for a lot of their time.

Compare:

"There's a 45-minute video presentation I'd like you to watch."

Versus:

"Do you have five minutes right now? Great, let me show you what this is all about."

Sizzle calls are a big time-saver. In fact, if you use them the way I do, in a few minutes, you can find out if a prospect is or isn't interested and either eliminate them (for now) and move onto other prospects, or move forward with them to the next step.

No more endless follow-ups to remind them to watch your video or dial into your conference call. No more endless follow-ups to find out if they are interested.

In five minutes, you know.

One way to use sizzle calls is to give the number to prospects as one of several options they can look at. For example, you might give them links to a few online videos, some articles about your products and company, your distributor website, the log-in page for your upcoming webinar, your weekly conference call number, AND the sizzle call phone number.

The distributor decides what to look at. Giving them several options increases the chances that they will look at *something*.

This works. I've done this, too. But I primarily use sizzle calls as a sorting tool, to weed out prospects who aren't interested and quickly find those who are.

Using sizzle calls this way has made a huge difference in my recruiting, simply because I get more prospects looking at some information.

How do I get prospects to listen?

I started out giving them the phone number for the sizzle call. I'd ask them to dial and listen to the message and I would call them to see what they thought. Or I asked them to call me back.

This worked, but I still found myself wasting time playing phone tag with prospects who didn't call the number or take my call when I followed up. That's when I found another way.

Here's how I described this in my book, *Recruit and Grow Rich*:

TWO WAYS TO USE SIZZLE CALLS

(1) GAPPING

The first way to use a sizzle call is to give the phone number to the prospect and ask them to call. It's called "GAPPING" because you tell them to "G.A.P." (Grab a Pen) and you give them the number.

Gapping allows you to do a thirty-second exposure: "Hey Bob, I've got something I want you to listen to. Grab a pen and write this down—555-333-5353. It's a recorded message, and it's just five minutes. Dial that number and listen and I'll call you back in six minutes to see what you think, okay?"

If they ask what it's about, say something like, "That takes all the fun out of it; it's only five minutes. Go ahead and call and I'll call you back."

Of course in the digital world, you don't have to ask them to grab a pen, you can text them the number. This allows you to do a **seven-second exposure**: "Hey Bob, I'm going to text you a phone number I'd like to you call. It's a five minute recorded message. Dial the number and I'll call you in six minutes, okay?"

GAPPING allows you to expose a lot of people quickly. In an hour, you can get twenty or thirty people agreeing to listen to information about your business. Your directness and the urgency in your voice make them curious to find out what out what's on that recording.

You can also GAP a prospect after you have piqued their interest or asked for a favor (opinion or referrals). After they have agreed to look at some information, you might say:

YOU: Do you have six minutes right now?

PROSPECT: Yes. (If they don't, don't give them the number; ask them when they will have six minutes and call back.)

YOU: Great! Grab a pen and write down this number: 555-333-5353. Got it? Okay, this is a five-minute recorded message that tells you what we do and how we make money. Call that number and I'll call you back in six minutes, okay?"

(2) THREE-WAY TO THE SIZZLE CALL

When you GAP someone, even though you're only asking for a few minutes, not surprisingly, they don't always make the call. They may be busy and forget. They may write down the wrong number. They may get interrupted.

When I started in the business, I GAPPED a lot of prospects and found that when I called back, many still hadn't listened to the call. Or I got their voicemail. They were at work and I understood that they had other things to do but I grew frustrated calling back and leaving several messages just to get them to make the call, or to find out if they had.

I decided that it was better to spend a few minutes while I had them on the phone and find out immediately if they were interested. I did this by three-way calling them to the recording and listening with them.

First, I asked if they had the time before I told them what I planned to do. "Do you have five minutes right now?" If they did, I did the three-way. If they didn't, I set up a time when I could call them back.

If they had the time, I explained what I was doing: "Okay, what I'm going to do is three-way conference us into a recorded messagethat shows you [what we do and how we make money]. It's about five minutes long. You might want to get a piece of paper and take notes or write down questions. Okay, I'm going to put you on hold for just a few seconds and then I'll come back on and the message will start playing. . . Hold on. . ."

At the end of the call, I know that (a) they heard the message, and (b) they are either interested or they are not.

I don't have to call back to find out. No leaving messages, no phone tag, no wondering. In five minutes, I know.

Yes, it takes longer to three-way prospects into the call and listen to it with them, but in an hour, I can almost always get more exposures done by three-way calling prospects to a sizzle call than I can by GAPPING.

5-MINUTE RECRUITING

Recruiting distributors using nothing but a sizzle call isn't the norm, but it is possible. I've done it and you can too.

It's easier when:

- The prospect trusts and respects you
- They're already a customer and believe in the products
- The cost to get started is reasonable

In addition, you'll need a sizzle call that persuades them that

(a) they can "do" what you do,

(b) they will have the time to do it, and

(c) it will be worth it.

"Worth it" means different things to different people. Some want to earn some extra income, some want to get rich. Some want to share your great products with the world, some want to work from home.

Whatever it is they want, your message (and what you say to them) have to show them that getting it is possible.

Most of the distributors I've signed up with just a sizzle call were fellow professionals who either knew me or knew my reputation. They respected me and when I showed them what I was doing (via my story and a sizzle call), they saw what I saw and wanted what I wanted.

They had questions. Your prospects will, too. Questions are good. They mean they're interested.

For basic questions, e.g., Where do I sign up, How much do I earn when someone buys X?, or After I sign up, what's the next step, go ahead and answer.

For more involved questions (or objections), 3-way call them to a third-party "expert" to answer and "close" them.

If they have a seemingly endless list of questions, you can do what I do. I answer a few questions and then tell them, "That will be covered in your training."

When you offer the right opportunity to the right prospect, that may be all you need to get them to say yes.

Most prospects, even the most excited ones, won't sign up after just a sizzle call. On the other hand, why not assume that they will? Ask them if they're ready to get started. You might be pleasantly surprised at their response.

You can use sizzle calls with any kind of prospect (warm market, purchased leads, callers to your lead capture line, etc.)

In your warm market, the easiest way to get prospects to listen is to ask for a favor. Ask them to listen to the message and give you their opinion (about what's on the message) or to listen and tell you if they know anyone who might be interested.

After they hear the message, ask them what they liked best. If they liked *anything,* give them your website, invite them to a conference call or an in-person event, or do a sit-down. Or ask them if they're ready to get started.

If they didn't like anything (and don't have any referrals), move on.

In the cold market, although it's possible to ask for a favor, it's usually best to pique the prospect's interest before doing the exposure. Tell them a little about what you do and then either GAP them or 3-way them to the message.

You can also use a sizzle call during a sit down with a prospect. Instead of investing 45 minutes showing them a video or doing a flip chart presentation only to find out they're not interested, take 5 minutes, dial-up your message and hand them the phone (or put it on speaker).

When you have a prospect in the car with you and you're on the way to an event (but you haven't yet done an exposure), play the sizzle call for them to give them a preview.

And when you meet someone and they ask, "What do you do?" ask if they have five minutes and if they do, dial up the call for them to listen.

For more on how to pique a prospect's interest and how to do exposures, follow-ups and close, see *Recruit and Grow Rich.*

PART IV

GETTING PROSPECTS TO CALL YOU BACK

CHAPTER 8: HOW TO LEAVE A VOICEMAIL MESSAGE THAT GETS PROSPECTS TO CALL YOU BACK

How much time do you spend following-up with prospects who don't answer their phone and don't call you back?

Yeah, a lot.

Since so few prospects call you back, have you ever asked yourself if you should even bother leaving a message? Maybe you should use that time calling other prospects.

When you do leave a message, have you ever tried to figure out what to say to get them to call you back?

In this chapter, I'm going to share my thoughts about what to do in several common situations. I'll give you the options as I see them and share my recommendations.

FIRST CALL TO WARM MARKET PROSPECTS

You haven't spoken to them or sent them anything. They don't know what you do. This is your first call.

Option A: No message

Assuming you're in their phone's contact list, many prospects will see your name on caller ID and call you back, even if you don't leave a message. If they don't, call them again. If you still don't reach them, you can either leave a message (see Option B) or call again at another time.

Option B: Leave the same message you would leave for them if you were calling them for any other reason

"Hey Bob, it's David. Give me a call when you get a chance."

Or

"Hey Bob, it's David. I want to run something by you. Give me a call when you get this message".

Or

"Hey Bob, it's David Ward. I haven't spoken to you in a long time and I was wondering how you're doing and what you're up to these days. Give me a call and let's get caught up. My number is. . . "

And that's it. Don't tell them what you want to talk to them about or go on about how important it is or how excited you are. Be normal.

If they text or message you back instead of calling, reply and tell them you can't type that fast and ask them to call, or just call them.

CALLING PROSPECTS WHO LEFT A MESSAGE ON YOUR LEAD CAPTURE LINE

They've heard your lead capture message and left you a message. They want your free report and/or expect you to contact them.

This one is easy. On your first call to these prospects, you should always leave a message. Identify yourself, refer to the message they left you (on your lead capture system) and ask them to call you back.

Something like this:

"Hi, this is Donna Distributor. I'm calling Peter Prospect. Peter, you recently listened to a message I recorded and asked me to contact you about [a business you can work from home/learning how to solve (a problem your product addresses)/etc.]. I need to speak with you for a few minutes to find out [what you had in mind/how serious things are/what you've done before], and see if there's a good fit for what I have for you. You can reach me at xxx-xxx-xxxx. If you get my voicemail when you call, tell me the best times to reach you. Again, that's Donna Distributor, and my number is xxx-xxx-xxxx. I look forward to speaking with you."

FIRST CALL TO COLD MARKET PROSPECTS

This is your first call to purchased leads or other cold market prospects (not including prospects who called your message line).

Option A: No message

Statistically, since so few people will call you back, leaving a message truly may not be the best use of your time. If you choose this option, make a note of the day and time you called and call them again at a different time.

Option B: Regular message

If you choose to leave a message, you want to sound business-like, confident, and get right to the point:

"Hi Mr. Jones, this is Donna Distributor getting back to you with the information you requested [about starting a business, working from home, etc.]. It's Thursday, December 10th. Please call me back today [or, "no later than tomorrow night"]. You can reach me until six pm at xxx-xxx-xxxx. Again, my name is Donna Distributor and my number is xxx-xxx-xxxxx. Talk to you soon."

Here's another option (for purchased leads):

"Hi Mr. Jones, this is Donna Distributor getting back to you with the information you requested about working from home. You're going to receive

multiple calls from different people with different companies. We are not the same. As you know, when you start a home-based business, it's important to align yourself with a winning team and a winning leader and you'll find that with me. So if you're serious, call me back right away at xxx-xxx-xxxx."

Since most prospects won't call you back after your first message, the purpose of leaving this message is to set the stage for your next call. If they are screening calls, for example, they might now pick up the phone because they recognize your name and liked something you said. Who knows, they might even call you back.

Experiment with different messages. Try a more friendly message. Try a message where you say something unusual or funny. Try a message with more information, or less. Keep track of the messages you use with each prospect and see which gets the best response.

Option C: "One and Done"

You don't have to talk to every lead. You don't have to recruit every prospect. It's your business and you can do what you want.

If you get a prospect's voicemail and they sound weak or unprofessional or you otherwise don't want to spend a lot of time talking to them, instead of leaving a "regular" message asking them to call you back (Option B), *and instead of calling them again,* tell them why you called (e.g., they filled out a form seeking information about starting a business, etc.), and give them your website and/or your sizzle call number, and your phone number, and move on:

"Take a look at the website (or, listen to the call) and call me back within 24 hours if you are interested/want more information."

Or...

"After you watch the video (or, listen to the message), if you're interested in the business and feel you are the type of person we're looking to work with, I'll need you to call me back so we can discuss your qualifications in more detail, okay? My name again is... And my number is xxx-xxx-xxxx".

Or...

"After you watch the video on the website, you can get started by clicking the "Get Started" link at the top of the page. Once you've signed up, I'll contact you to help you get things going. If you have any questions, give me a call at xxx-xxx-xxxx."

In other words, put "the next step" in their hands and you're done. If they sign up, work with them. If they don't sign up or contact you, don't contact them again, at least by phone. You can do that via email (e.g., put them on a drip campaign), but you're done calling them, at least for now.

Option D: They sound sharp and you want to talk to them

You hear their voicemail message. They sound sharp. You want to talk to them. Leave a regular message (Option B).

Option E: voicemail Drop

If you're cold calling, instead of leaving a "call me back" message, another option is to leave a voicemail directing the prospect to your lead capture message line. See Chapter 6 regarding what to say on your message.

COLD MARKET PROSPECTS YOU'VE NEVER SPOKEN TO

Whenever you call prospects you're previously called but never spoken to, instead of leaving a "call me back" message, you have another option. It's similar to the "voicemail Drop" above, but instead of directing them to your lead capture message (you already have their name and number), you direct them to a sizzle call:

"There's a recorded message [or I've recorded a message] that tells you what this is all about. It's just 5 minutes. The number for that message is xxx-xxx-xxxx. Give that a call and I'll call you Friday to answer your questions. If you want to speak to me sooner, you can reach me at xxx-xxx-xxxx."

"One and Done" option: "...Call the message and if you like what you hear, call me at xxx-xxx-xxxx and I'll show you a way to earn $1,000 in your first ten days."

Note, it's always better to speak to prospects before you do an exposure. You want to find out what they want, make a connection, build some trust, and get them to focus on what you are about to show them. But if you can't reach them and they don't call you back, this gives you the option to move things forward.

FOLLOW-UP CALL TO PHONE APPOINTMENTS

I strongly suggest that whenever you speak with a prospect, at the end of the call you schedule the next conversation. In other words, schedule a "phone appointment"—the date and time when you will call them again.

When I call someone with whom I've scheduled a phone appointment and they don't answer, I leave a message like this:

"It's David Ward. It's 4 O'clock on Thursday. We have a phone appointment scheduled at this time. I'm guessing you're running a couple minutes late so call me as soon as you get this. If something came up and you can't talk, no problem; call me and we'll re-schedule. I'm at xxx-xxx-xxxx. I look forward to speaking with you".

If they don't call me back to keep the appointment or re-schedule it, I don't call them again. We had an appointment. If they're not responsible enough to keep their promises, I don't want them in my business.

For more on handling follow-ups, see *Recruit and Grow Rich*.

FOLLOW-UP CALL AFTER MULTIPLE CALLS/MESSAGES

You've spoken to a cold market prospect (a lead or a prospect who called your lead capture message) and you've done one or more exposures. You've left more than a few messages for them but they're not calling you back.

Option A: Different benefits on each message

Each time you leave a message, highlight a different benefit: income, time freedom, work for yourself, work from home, training/support, low startup costs, product benefits, etc. If possible, illustrate the benefit with a story. ("I'm working with a guy who...")

They might hear something they didn't pick up on before or you might be reaching them at a time when they really need to hear about that benefit. Telling them about someone who was previously in the same situation and found the solution with your business or product might be exactly what they need to hear.

All of a sudden, they're ready to talk.

But don't chase. Never chase. You don't need them and you should never sound like you do. You're simply pointing out things they need to know before they make up their mind.

Option B: "This is the last time I'll call you..."

If they're not calling you back, do a "takeaway". Tell them you won't be calling again and if they are at all serious about [the benefit they told you they wanted], they have to call *you*.

You want them to understand that they need you more than you need them. Leave your name and number but do it with a bit of "resignation" in your voice.

Option C: The nuclear option

After several exposures and follow-up conversations, if they tell you they're still interested but they have one excuse after another as to why they can't get started, there is one last thing you can try. You can make them an offer they can't refuse:

"Hi Mr. Jones, I've got some news for you. I just signed up a new distributor, Mr. Bigpants, and he's a real firecracker. He's got a huge list and a lot of experience in the industry. I know he's going to build a BIG business and help a lot of people make a lot of money. That's where you come in. If you're still interested in joining the team, let me know and I'll put Mr. Bigpants

under you. He'll be on your team and all of those overrides will go to you. But I have to place him today [tomorrow/by Friday at Noon] so I need to hear from you by 5 pm or I'll have to put him somewhere else. Call me. The number is xxx-xxx-xxx. Remember, 5 pm is the cutoff..."

If they are at all serious about the business, how could they not call you back?

WHAT ABOUT PROSPECTS WHO SCREEN THEIR CALLS?

There isn't a lot you can do about prospects who screen *all* of their calls. If they don't pick up when you call, you either leave a message or you don't. Many people don't screen all calls, however, and there are a couple of things you can do to improve the odds that a prospect will answer, which means you won't have to leave a message.

First, if you don't have caller ID enabled on your phone, you should do so. Many people don't answer calls that come from "unidentified callers".

Also, see if you can make your caller ID display your first and last name, not just your phone number. Prospects are more likely to answer the phone when they recognize your name, or they see that a "regular" person is calling and not a telemarketer from a company trying to sell them something.

Second, as I mentioned earlier, always note the day and time of day you call each prospect. If a prospect doesn't answer the phone at a certain time of day, call at a different time. Keep trying different times and days to see if you can catch them.

Conventional wisdom says not to call too early or too late but you may want to experiment with that. They may not be in the best mood if you call them when they are asleep or eating dinner, but it might be better to have them answer in a bad mood than not answer at all.

ON EVERY MESSAGE

Leave your number every time, including area code, and *repeat* it. (Never assume they have your number.)

Say your name clearly and spell it.

Don't say anything important after you state your name and number. They might think you have finished leaving the message and hang up without hearing you mention your time zone, the best time to reach you, or other important information.

PART V

QUICK START GUIDE

QUICK START GUIDE

You've learned how recorded messages can help you grow your business, how to create effective scripts, how to record messages, and how to use your messages to get more leads and recruit more distributors. Now it's time to get to work.

Here is a summary of what to do:

LEAD CAPTURE MESSAGE

(1) Set up a free account with SimpleVoiceBox.com

Take a few minutes to learn how to use the controls. Record a 30 second "outgoing" test message and listen to the playback.

(2) Create an incentive to offer prospects.

If you plan to offer a free report or other material to prospects as an incentive for leaving their contact information, see if your company or upline team has something you can use. Or start gathering articles and other information to create your own "report".

(3) Write your lead capture script.

Re-read the sample lead capture message scripts in this book. See if your company or other distributors have a lead capture message you can listen to. Record and transcribe these messages. Re-read Chapter 2 and write your lead capture message script.

(4) Record your message.

Follow the instructions in Chapter 5 to record your message. Ask some friends to call and leave you a message. Make sure they are able to hear everything. When you know your message line is working, start promoting it.

(5) Promote your message number.

Start by posting the number (and offer) on social media and anywhere else you currently promote your business.

When you're ready, promote your lead capture message number. See Chapter 6.

Track your numbers. How many calls are you getting? How many callers listen to the entire message? How many leave a message for you? Tweak your message script and see if you can improve your numbers.

(6) Expand and grow your numbers.

Once you know your lead capture message works, look for more places to advertise and promote it. If you use pay-per-click ads, select additional keywords, increase your bids and/or daily budget.

(7) Help your distributors set up their own lead capture messages.

Show your distributors how to do what you've done. Help them set up and use their own lead capture message.

SIZZLE CALL MESSAGE

As mentioned earlier, if you have access to good sizzle calls recorded by other distributors, use them. You may not need to record your own call(s), at least not anytime soon.

When you *are* ready to record your own call or calls, follow these steps:

(1) Gather raw materials.

Record and transcribe existing sizzle calls used by other distributors in your company and gather additional information (notes, ideas, bullet points, etc.), as described in Chapter 4.

(2) Write your sizzle call script.

Don't copy anyone else's script (unless you have permission), use their scripts as models or templates for writing your own.

(3) Record your message or ask someone else to record it.

See Chapter 5.

(4) Start using it with your prospects.

GAP and/or 3-way prospects into your call. Track your numbers. See which method lets you (a) do more exposures and (b) recruit more distributors.

Let others on your team use your sizzle call message.

(5) Track your numbers and improve your message.

Are you getting prospects to tell you they're interested? How many? How does this compare to what you've done in the past?

Is your team using your message? If not, ask them why. Are they using another message? Why? How is that message better than yours? What can you do to improve your message? Re-write and re-record your message (if necessary).

(6) Record additional sizzle call messages.

Modify your script and record additional messages for different niche markets. Or ask someone on your team to do it.

OTHER MESSAGES

Recorded messages are easy to record and easy to use. Once you've recorded one or two, you'll know to do it and you'll be able to record more messages:

- Lead capture messages for specific niche markets (in addition to sizzle calls)
- Lead capture and sizzle calls for product sales
- Testimonial or "closing" messages
- Training messages

When your company announces new products, a new comp plan, or a big promotion, record a new message. As your team grows, update your sizzle call to feature their stories, or record additional messages.

ABOUT THE AUTHOR

David M. Ward is an attorney, business owner, marketing consultant, and author.

Ward started in network marketing to build retirement income and to escape the long hours of his law practice. "I was a victim of the self-employment trap—trading my time for dollars," he says. "The bigger my practice grew, the harder I had to work."

After twenty years, he was ready for a change. "Network marketing gave me the time freedom and financial freedom I always wanted and allowed me to do things I never had the time to do when I was practicing law."

Ward has been recognized as a six-figure income earner and top recruiter in his network marketing company. He lives in southern California.

[a] amazon.com/author/dward

ALSO BY DAVID M WARD

Recruiting Up: How I Recruited Hundreds of Professionals in My Network Marketing Business and How You Can, Too

http://recruitingup.com

Recruit and Grow Rich: How to Quickly Build a Successful Network Marketing Business by Recruiting Smarter, Not Working Harder

http://recruitandgrowrichbook.com/kindle

Fix Your Network Marketing Business: Fire Up Your Team, Increase Recruiting and Sales, and Get Your Business Growing Again—Even if Nobody is Doing Anything

http://www.recruitandgrowrich.com/fix

Network Marketing Made Simple: A Guide For Training New Distributors

http://recruitandgrowrichbook.com/nmms

ONE LAST THING

Thank you for purchasing my book. If you found the information useful, please leave a **review**. Even one sentence helps.

Remember, to get more recruiting tips and special offers, subscribe to my **FREE Recruiting Tips Newsletter.**

Go here to subscribe:

http://recruitandgrowrich.com/newsletter

Finally, if you would like to send me your comments on this book, or suggestions for future books, please email me at recruitingbook@gmail.com

I'd love to hear from you.

—David M. Ward